Contents

About the author

Robbie Burns has been a journalist and writer since he graduated from Harlow Journalism College in 1981. After starting life as a reporter and editor for various local newspapers, from 1988-1992 he was editor of ITV and Channel 4's teletext services. He then went on to freelance for various newspapers including *The Independent* and *The Sun*, and also helped set up a financial news service for CNN. In 1997 he became editor for BSkyB's teletext services and set up their shares and finance service.

He left full-time work in 2001 to trade and run his own businesses. While at BSkyB, Robbie broadcast a diary of his share trades which became hugely popular. He transferred the diary to his website, www.nakedtrader.co.uk, which quickly became one of the most read financial websites in the UK. Between 2002 and 2005 he wrote a column for *The Sunday Times*, 'My DIY Pension', featuring share buys and sells made for his pension fund. He managed to double the money in his fund from £40,000 to £80,000 in under three years. He also writes a weekly column for the leading financial website, ADVFN.com.

Robbie has made a tax free profit of over £190,000 from trading shares since 1999, and has made a profit every year, even during the market downturn of 2000-2002.

He lives with his wife, Elizabeth, in Fulham, London, with son Christopher and cat Domino. His hobbies include chess, running, swimming, horse racing, and trading shares from his bedroom, erm... naked.

Acknowledgements

I dedicate this book to my wife Elizabeth. Every night she's heard me moan, "I've got to get on with that bloody book!" And every night she didn't complain when I ended up on the sofa with a bowl of rice pudding and the paper. She also helped enormously with the final editing of the book. I'd also like to say thanks to my newborn son Christopher for not being sick over my keyboard and just being gorgeous! Thanks also to my editor, Stephen Eckett, for his patience with my extremely slow progress.

Introduction

Ever wondered whether you could make money by buying and selling shares?

I think you can – whatever your age, job, status or character defects! And this book is going to be your best friend if you want to learn how to make money from shares. I'll reveal to you commonsense stock market knowledge that's taken me years to learn. You can learn from the things I've done right – and learn even more from the things I did wrong.

Learn from my early mistakes

You see, as the Naked Trader, I will reveal everything! I'm not going to pretend I've never made a mistake. In fact, I revel in mistakes. The point is to learn a lesson from them.

If you've never traded a share before it doesn't matter, as I'll guide you every step of the way. And if you have traded for a while and have made losses – I am confident I can put you on the road to long-term stock market success.

You won't find any inexplicable stock market jargon in this book – I write in plain English. You will not have to start scratching your head and think "what is he on about?" or "what the hell is a head and shoulders formation?" I'm going to explain how to buy and sell shares the easy way, and guide you to the winners. I'll be taking you through every step and explaining all the silly jargon.

The fact is stock market investment is easier than you think.

Brokers and tipsters love to spout the jargon because it makes them look clever and to persuade you to part with your hard-earned money from their 'advice'. But I'll guide you through all that nonsense so that *you* can make your own decisions and do your own research.

This is not a get rich quick book

One thing I certainly can't do is promise that £10,000 you have spare is going to become £100,000 overnight, because you've read the book and put my ideas into action. You know those ads 'Make £400 a day from the markets...', 'Become a stock market millionaire with our software...'. Come on, you know in your heart that when it sounds too good to be true – it is!

This book is about building your wealth slowly and surely – with realistic targets and time frames. Using discipline, good stock picking techniques and avoiding the mistakes new investors nearly always make, I believe I can make you richer.

Trading shares is an exciting roller-coaster ride with plenty of thrills and spills. I really hope that excitement comes over in *The Naked Trader*.

Who this book is for

This book is for both complete stock market beginners and those who have recently started trading or investing. However, I hope old hands will also find it useful and entertaining.

I was spurred into writing it when a friend asked me: "I'd like to buy some M&S shares, but I have no idea how to buy them or even if I should." I realised that I, and many others, learned how to buy shares by 'doing it for ourselves'. That means we all learned the hard way – by making loads of mistakes. There wasn't a book around that covered the real basics of stock market investment and also how to find the right shares and avoid the wrong ones. So I hope this book not only fills the gap, but will also continue to be an invaluable guide even when you have gained a lot of experience.

If you have never bought or sold a share before, I hope I'll arm you with the information you'll need to start trading. This includes everything from how to buy a share to getting real-time prices. Then I'll tell you everything I've learned over seven active years of trading. You'll learn what makes shares move and what to watch for before pressing that buy button. I can also reveal how to make money by backing shares to go *down*.

Whether you have a small amount to trade or you've inherited a hundred thousand, I hope after reading *The Naked Trader* you will be well armed to enter the fray.

So, get a cup of tea, put your feet up and welcome to the crazy world of shares.

1

Escaping The Rat Race

My story

I am out of the rat race.

I no longer have to go to the same office every day and do the same work so I can pay off my mortgage and all the other bills every month. I don't have to report to a boss and I'm master of my own destiny. No tedious Monday morning meetings with the same old people talking the same old rubbish!

I achieved this by developing multiple income streams – one of which happened to be making money by trading shares. Before we get onto the development of how I started to realise I had a knack for picking winning shares, let me explain how I also developed other methods of making money.

I realised one day that working for someone else was a bit of a mug's game. Whoever you worked for, they'd only pay you enough to keep you there. Even on a good salary, say £40,000, you were never going to be wealthy. After tax it wasn't that much, and even less after paying a mortgage and other living expenses.

As Dolly Parton put it:

> *"Working 9-5 what a way to make a living, it's enough to drive you crazy if you let it... ."*

My plan to escape the mug's game

So I developed a plan. That was to try and make money from sources other than my salaried job.

I worked on three sets of income:

1. share trading;

2. selling mobile phones and cheap home phone calls; and, er...

3. Buffy The Vampire Slayer.

Over time my actual full-time job wage became a tiny part of my overall income.

The profitable Buffy

Buffy might sound bizarre, but it ended up being my biggest money spinner.

I started a Buffy information line, where eager teenagers could discover what was coming next in the series. I kept a proportion of the proceeds, while my employer, BSkyB, also took a cut in return for advertising the service. The line, together with other TV info lines, built into a substantial income for little or no effort. I ended up with around £250,000 in profits from these lines by the time I left BSkyB. Of course tax took a fair chunk out of that!

Telecom Plus

The other income came from a stock market company called Telecom Plus. I became a part-time distributor for them after reading some junk mail I'd received. The idea was you sold a box which when plugged into a phone line would save a lot of money. In return for the sale Telecom Plus handed out some cash, but more importantly *residual income*. That is, a cut of every call made by the customer for as long as they were a customer. On top of that I could build a network of distributors under me, getting a cut of their sales too.

By 2001, I'd built a huge pile of money and my alternative incomes were paying big sums – way more than my salary. I was very bored with my full-time job by this stage. Staff were laid off and there was suddenly very little for me to do.

Hasta la vista rats

There was nothing to lose, so I decided it was time to quit the rat race!

I held on for six months because I was fairly certain I could grab a big redundancy cheque. I achieved this by irritating my boss as much as possible. He was a nice chap, so it was quite difficult, but it got me the cheque.

Armed, therefore, with a huge pile of cash, I bought a café business to provide a kind of safety net against trading losses. The Telecom Plus business pretty well ran itself, and I continue now to receive excellent income every month. The idea behind buying the café was to have a cash-generating business which would provide me with a stable income if share trading or other businesses went badly.

I'm now in the great position of really trading with money I can afford to lose. And that, I think, makes me a better investor.

Note

As a side note, if you too are interested in quitting the rat race, click onto my website www.nakedtrader.co.uk and read my 'Escape' piece.

How I started trading

My very first trade – I remember it well!

I was working for ITV's teletext service, then known as ORACLE. I edited feature material – most of it was abysmal stuff. The journalists there hated me because they'd never been edited before and took exception to changes to their copy. (Especially the one who snorted too much powder – his stories were really paranoid!)

The place needed some new ideas, so I started writing a daily soap opera called 'Park Avenue', which attracted a healthy audience. I also started running phone polls on the issues of the day (for example, "Should cannabis be legalised?" – it was usually 95% against, as the cannabis users were usually too stoned to phone in).

Still, I found the work rather easy and got bored at times. I wanted a bit of excitement. That's when I met the chap who ran the premium rate line phone company, which I decided to use for the phone polls. He was an entertaining guy – let's call him Tarquin – wealthy and very funny. He suggested I buy some shares, telling me how much money he'd made from the markets.

A sure-fire tip

As it happened, I did have £500 to spare. Tarquin suggested I put it in a drugs company called Bimec. So I set up a share trading account and duly bought the shares at 45p. I added them to the list of shares broadcast by ORACLE so I could watch their progress. Price movements (delayed by half an hour) were updated every 20 minutes.

I'd certainly found a way to get some excitement!

I found it really exciting whenever it went up half a penny – and *so* upsetting when it went down. In those days there was no internet, the only way to get close to real-time share prices was using teletext.

I could also call a premium rate line (Tarquin's, of course) to get the real-time price. A recorded tape said in a deep voice:

"Thank you for calling the real-time share price line"
[a ruse to keep you holding on and spending money.]

"Please enter the share code..."

"Bimec Industries. The price is... UP a quarter pence to.. 46 pence".

It really was quite addictive.

A stock market genius is born, but then...

I even started buying tipping magazines and wondering whether I should buy shares in other companies – because I was in profit on Bimec. I was obviously a bit of a stock market genius!

But before I started buying more shares, something put me off the stock market.

Bimec went bust.

I could hardly believe it. I'd lost the lot!

The lessons I learnt

In retrospect, losing money was possibly the best thing that could have happened to me. It forced me to learn some lessons. In my first trade I made many mistakes I'd never make now, such as:

- doing no research;
- buying on a tip;
- putting all my eggs in one basket;
- looking for excitement; and
- falling in love with the company.

The one thing I had done right was I'd invested money I could afford to lose.

The great thing about losing the lot with my very first trade was that it put me off investing – and I didn't return to the markets for several years. But when I did, I was already armed with the knowledge gained from this one trade.

About my trading

I have an absolutely great time trading!

I love the ups and downs, and the challenge of trying to be in the right share at the right time. I've managed to increase my wealth every year since 1999 – which is when I started to trade seriously – even during the bear years of 2000 and 2001.

Trades made for my website (www.nakedtrader.co.uk) show profits, as I write, of more than £150,000 since I started in 1999. However, my total investments including those not mentioned on the site show profits of £190,000 – completely free of tax thanks to ISAs and spread betting tax rules (explained later).

And, although I enjoy making the profits and steadily increasing my wealth, trading is also a great intellectual challenge. It keeps me mentally fit!

Day trading is not for me

My kind of trading is *not* that of what is termed a 'day trader'. I would class myself as a *frequent trader*. It's really more investing than trading, although the difference between the two is not as great as many people think.

Day trading does not interest me – it's far too difficult and I don't have the concentration. I prefer buying and selling somewhere between once and five times a week. It means I don't always have to be looking at a screen every minute of the day – I want to enjoy my days. I don't fancy sitting in front of a computer screen all the time – I may as well go back to having a full-time job! Frequent trading gives me the freedom to: go for a coffee with friends; pop out for a swim; relax with a cup of tea and the papers; or enjoy a bit of quality time with my son, even sometimes watch daytime TV (isn't Judy looking tired!).

What I hope you'll learn is that you don't need to spend 40 hours a week in front of a screen. And you can still have a full-time job and make money from the markets, as long as you have access to the internet.

2

A Day In The Life Of A Naked Trader

Dear diary...............

6am

Woken up rudely by the sound of a giant plane overhead. Yes, it's Fulham, London, and we're on the flight path. Still, make the most of it and get up. Have some breakfast and feed the cat (who just licks the jelly off the food and leaves the meat).

Go to living room with breakfast and The Sun, The Times, The Mail, and the Investors Chronicle. Turn on Bloomberg. Turn off Bloomberg - it's all that boring stuff about Asian markets. Read The Sun. Takes about 90 seconds, but it eases me into the day. Then get stuck into The Times - it has a pretty good business section and I catch up on news I may have missed yesterday. A couple of shares look interesting and I make a note to have a look at them later.

7.15am

Back to bed with the laptop. Careful to be quiet as Elizabeth is still soundly asleep. Companies reporting their results generally release the announcements around this time, so I have a gander through some of the news stories on ADVFN. I see two companies I have open positions on have reported this morning: Dignity and BSkyB.

Dignity is a funeral parlour chain and reports 'deaths are down by 6%'. That doesn't look good! But the rest of the report looks fine. It should go up. Wonder if I get a free coffin upgrade for being a shareholder?

The BSkyB report is not so good, but that's great as I have a short open (that means I will make money if the share price goes down). It should open lower and it may be worth closing my position for a profit.

Have a look at the Investors Chronicle. Yipee - they've tipped one of my holdings: Vanco. This usually means an instant rise in the shares before the market opens, as market makers know there will be buy orders coming in and they can raise the offer price immediately. Sometimes, if there's a share I want to take a profit on and it's been tipped, I sell into the strength generated by the tip to get out. However, I like Vanco's business model and agree with the Investors Chronicle's recommendation.

7.30am

Check to see if any new emails have come in from my website readers. Two spam mails wondering if I'd like a bigger willie. No, perfectly happy, thanks. Well, Mrs Naked hasn't got any complaints. Delete.

Some readers want reassurance that the dodgy tech shares they've bought aren't going to tumble any further. Politely reply that I can't advise them.

Two readers want more info on how to become Telecom Plus distributors, because they want to quit the rat race like me. I copy them details. One also has a 'good' share tip, that I wouldn't touch with a bargepole. I reply kindly to him though. I'm not allowed to give advice on specific shares, as I'm not a regulated tipster. When I'm emailed for advice, I have to say I can't. They understand. I'd rather not anyhow.

One reader has an interesting warning about dealing in covered warrants and tells me to be careful - it's a good email and I put it in pending-to-reply-later folder.

Finally, one reader tells me where I can get three cans of creamed rice for the price of two as, for some reason, I was discussing creamed rice pudding on the site yesterday.

7.45am

Grab some tea and toast for the missus and scan the business pages of the Daily Mail before handing it over to her. Relax in bed with the laptop.

8am

The market opens - always an exciting time.

It's interesting to see which shares the market makers have

marked up or down, without any trades at all going through. I check through my watchlist and all looks fine - nothing dramatic is going on.

The market obviously liked Dignity's statement as the shares are up 4p. My short of BSkyB is now showing a profit of more than £1,000 as the shares sink fast. Time to take profits?

The Footsie (FTSE 100 Index) starts the day down. Happy with that too as I've got a Footsie short open. Vanco is marked up 2p, thanks to the Investors Chronicle tip. One of my favourite shares at the moment, VP Group, is also up a penny. On the downside, Serco, that I bought at 190 and hope to exit at 220, is down 2p. But the spread is wide (the difference between the buying and selling prices) and it's still early.

Some shares don't move at all for a while at this time of day and there's nothing much happening.

The worst feeling in the world is if a share you hold issues a profit warning and dives 40% before you can do anything about it. Fortunately, that hasn't happened to me for a long time!

I take look at the biggest percentage losers and winners of the day. I see a company called Ultraframe has issued a third profit warning and is down 12%. I do wonder, though, whether it could be a recovery play soon and therefore add it to my watchlist.

8.30am

Mrs Naked finishes the Daily Mail and asks how the market's going. "Not bad, a bit quiet," I reply. "Fancy a cuddle then?", she asks. You see - one of the perks of being self-employed! (You can mind your own business about what happens in the next three minutes - er, I mean half an hour.)

8.33 9.00am

Mrs Naked gets ready to go to the café we own round the corner. It's a great little business, and also a lot of fun to own your own café. I retrieve the laptop from under the bed. The cat comes out of hiding (she hates it when we cuddle). She leaps onto the laptop

- nearly buying a disastrous penny share with a wide spread. She enjoys watching me trade.

I run down my watchlist again, and all seems good. The market is on the slide, but my shares are holding up OK. VP continues its rise, as does Dignity, while BSkyB continues to slide. Vanco up 4p. Footsie still sinking.

Have a break: some tea and toast and a read of the Daily Mail.

10.10am

The phone rings. "Great news, you have won a prize...". Put the phone down. What do they think I am, an idiot?

10.15am

The market often goes quiet around this time, so it's off to the nearby gym on my bike for a good swim. Part of the joy of frequent trading, rather than day trading, is I don't have to sit in front of the screen all day. What's the point - it would be like having a job again. There's a slow breast-stroke lady dawdling in the fast lane. Dash past her and kick hard so she gets splashed. Did I tell you I was a ruthless Naked Trader?

My gym wants £550 for another year's membership. I bluff and say I was thinking of changing to another gym and could they offer me a cheaper deal? No, they could offer me four free guest passes. Time for a big bluff: "Oh well, I've liked it here but if you can't offer me anything...". The assistant disappears and has a chat with the manager. Result! One month's free membership and eight guest passes. Amazing what you can do when you haggle.

11am

Another look at the markets.

The Footsie is still heading south, which is good news as I have a lot of spread bet shorts open. My portfolio is doing OK. BSkyB shares still going down and the (paper) profits are rolling in.

Begin some preparation for my Sunday Times column. This week it's about covered warrants and house prices. I'm interested in making money on London house prices going down within my pension fund. I reckon I sold my house at the top of the market recently; I'm now renting as I believe prices will sink 20% in the next two or three years.

11.15am

BSkyB hits another low. Profits are currently £1,200 - good enough for me! I call Cantor Index and make a 'buy' of the shares to close out my short position. Great, profit banked! Now keep BSkyB on my list to consider going long (a straightforward buy) if the shares fall much further.

Suddenly notice one of my favourite shares, Sondex, has just gone up a penny. Check the level 2 on the share and see one of the market makers, Winterfloods, has actually raised its price by 3p. The other market makers look set to follow. I have exposure to £7,000 worth of stock, which was bought at 160p. The shares are now 204p to buy with two market makers. I already have a good profit, but Sondex has a niche market supplying oil drilling equipment and I think the shares have further to go. Make a quick decision and go to my broker's website. I have £6,000 in cash left in my ISA. Decide to put in an order to buy another 2,000 shares, with a limit of 205p in case they head up too quickly while I'm waiting. My order goes straight onto the market. My broker beats the price and gets me 203.5p. It looks like my order wakes up the other market makers and they quickly lift the price. Looks promising!

I take a look at ADVFN's Toplists to see if I can find any promising buy or shorting candidates. Look at the biggest percentage losers and gainers. Then a look though 52 and 12 week chart breakouts up and down. There's an interesting company called Alumasc, which I'd never heard of before; it's making a 12 week high. The price is 142-147 and I notice some big buys coming in at 145.5. Have a look at the chart. Looks promising. See results are due soon - could this buying be significant? Do more reading up about the company, but I'm simply not sure. I put it on my watchlist to keep an eye on for the future.

11.35am

Fancy a coffee so nip round to my café (one minutes walk away). My lovely wife has popped out to do some shopping. Let's hope she took cash and not her credit card! Have a cappuccino in my hand and just about to walk home, when one of the staff says a customer "wants to see the manager". Oh bum! "Can I help you?", I ask a rather scruffy looking woman sitting at a table with her boyfriend opposite who looked a bit embarrassed. "There are prawns in the fish pie and I'm allergic to them," she said. "I could end up in hospital this afternoon." In my best John Cleese impersonation mode I said: "So, madam, let me get this right. You are complaining because we have fish in our fish pie!" "It's prawns," she said. "Prawns are fish," I said, "and they are also very colourful and you can see them in the fish pie a mile away. And if I was allergic to any kind of fish I would just ask which fish were in the pie!" "I want a refund," she retorted, "you ought to put a sign up." "What?" I said, "Warning: There is fish in the fish pie!" Honestly! "Look, I'll give you a refund on the understanding you never set foot in here again." Now that might sound harsh, but she made the place look like a mess anyway. And I've always wanted to bar someone.

Nip home and have the coffee in the garden and a bit of a sunbathe.

Noon

Time to write my daily website update. The length of the updates has grown recently and it's taking me longer and longer. Readers seem to enjoy reading my ridiculous ramblings alongside the trading I talk about.

I kick off with a story about a big break-up at the café the other day. The café is known for its entertaining scenes between customers. This time, the bloke wanted the relationship to continue, even though she was seeing someone else. "You can see us both", he wailed. It was no good - she was off, and he ended up with a parking ticket. The whole café pretended to be reading the papers, of course. A lady told me, "You don't get this sort of thing at Starbucks".

I then gave a few replies to readers, I reviewed a new book, and then told them about my Sondex buy, BSkyB profit, and what a good day it generally was.

It took half an hour, not bad, and emailed it off to Dale, my webmaster, who updates the site for me in return for a pittance. It usually goes on air about half an hour after I write it.

12.30pm

Time for lunch!

The busiest time at the café - if it's really busy I might help out. But not today. Elizabeth is taking care of things, so I have a big plate of bacon and eggs. The cat helps me eat the bacon. A quick look at the markets and then a quick kip. Now you can't do that at the office can you?

12.55pm

Woken up by a dodgy company trying to sell me shares. "I have a great share called Motion Media. It's trading at 12p, but we can get you shares cheaper than the market", says the salesman. "I think Motion Media is a duff penny share," I said, having done some research on this company in the past. I then ask him if he is FSA registered, and whether he thinks it's legal to offer share tips over the phone. He starts to sound anxious. "What's the name of your company and what's your name?" I ask. Funny - the phone goes dead! (A few days later Motion Media is suspended and subsequently returns to the market at 4p!)

1pm

A friend calls to discuss his shares. He's a bit grumpy as, in his own words, "My ups are down and my downs are up!".

Put the news on in the background while I settle in front of the screen for a session. Sondex continues its climb up - great! BSkyB continues down - not so great, took profits too early! The Footsie is down 40, which means I'm up nearly 80 points on my Footsie down bet, which at a fiver a point is £400 profit. It's getting near the bottom of the current range. Maybe take profits today.

Although the Footsie is down, my smaller shares seem to be climbing. One in particular, VP, bought at 130p, has rocketed to over 160p. But with a low PE and an excellent statement I think there may be more rises to come. I do try and run my winners these days. I look at the chart and I reckon it could keep going to at least 200p. It's now up 2p on the day.

I notice a share that I made a lot of money on in the past, Retail Decisions, has fallen back today. I bought at 7p and sold at 18p not so long ago. It's down to 14p, which is quite a strong support level. There's some kind of lawsuit mooted against it by a rival. While tempted to buy in again, I decide to hold off and wait for the next statement from the company as shares have been weak.

1.30pm

Nothing much happening so decide to have a run on my treadmill. A healthy mind in a healthy body, as they say. Actually I find doing some sport every day clears the mind and helps with trading. Flick through the various music channels. My favourites at the moment are Toxic by Britney Spears (yes, I know!) and Satellite by Lou Reed.

2pm

Have a shower. Nip to the café to grab a cappuccino. We had a good lunchtime apparently with queues out of the door. We also rent DVDs and I see Something's Gotta Give with Jack Nicholson has just arrived. Grab it in case we fancy watching a movie tonight.

2.15pm

Back to the laptop.

Vanco and VP rising very nicely now. Serco not going so well and is now down 4p, but still above my buy price. Another share,

Fenner, starts to go down, but it's still above 100p, and I bought at 86p so feel quite relaxed about it.

My shorts are blossoming with the market sinking: shorts in Close Brothers, Pearson and 3i are all going well. I start to look around for other shorting opportunities, as I feel the Footsie is set to drop further over the next few weeks with interest rates rising and the oil price soaring. I notice Punch Taverns has broken down through a one year price range. The chart looks terrible. I look at the sector and remember pubs are doing really badly. People are staying at home drinking. Many profit warnings from the sector. I reckon the share could sink another 40p easily. Price is 445-446. Call up Cantor and ask for their spread price. 445-448. Not too bad. I sell for £12 a point at 445.

2.30pm

It's a nice afternoon, so I pop into the garden for a lie down in the sun. Trading takes it out of you!

3pm

Back to the computer with more tea and toast. The cat wakes up and demands some lunch. She then retires to bed again.

Looks like my short in Punch is well-timed with the shares down 5p since I sold them. Sondex continues to show strength. Vanco up another 2p, and VP going well. Fenner starts to climb after an initial fall. Serco still disappointing and refusing to go up. Many other shares stuck doing nothing.

3.30pm

My sister phones. She is big in the theatre world and tells me she's trying to keep a well known actor out of the tabloids. He's starring in one of her plays but has a penchant for lap dancers and worse. Trying to keep all this quiet from his wife is proving a tough job.

4pm

Rudely interrupted by the next-door neighbour who complains that my cat is crapping on her roof. She grimly shows the evidence

- a bag containing what does look like a large number of cat turds. I tell her the cat is 105 years old and I can't really stop her, but I promise to send someone up there once in a while to clear up the poos. She doesn't look convinced. Anyway I think she looks down on me - I'm sure she wonders why I'm in for most of the day wearing scruffy clothes. I think she regards me as a dodgy geezer.

4.30pm

The market closes.

The last five minutes is always interesting as the spreads move about quite a lot on the larger shares. It's been quite a good day, especially for the shorts. The Footsie has rallied a bit, but still finishes 30 points lower (£150 profit for me).

Punch Taverns finishes at 434, so I've already made about £120 from the trade today. Sondex ends at 225, a rise of ten % on the day, around £400 profit for me. My shorts have performed well. So, considering the markets are down today, it's been a good day overall. I make a note the Dow is down 50 - the difference between now and its close often makes the direction clear for the markets the next day.

Have a look at my accounts at the end of day. Just noticed a nice dividend has been paid for £210 from Telecom Plus - dividends certainly help to build up a fund! A nice £8,000 has built up in my spread betting account (mainly shorts). Meanwhile, money built up in my ISA and PEP is steadily rising.

Of course, the higher the profits I make, the more volatile the sum becomes. Just a small shift in value for all my shares would mean that sum going up, or down, £3,000 just like that. But I'm very lucky. I never even consider any of the money is mine and I can afford to lose it all. My aim for the next year or so is try and improve my total by 20%-30%. I do feel I could be a lot more disciplined with my stop losses and, if I can stamp out my weakness of holding onto losers for too long, I will make much more.

6pm

Elizabeth arrives home holding a video tape in her hand. "One of the staff is stealing," she said. "Is it my turn to sack someone or yours?" I asked. I had to sack the last one, who happened to have a black belt at karate. I carefully moved the office desk so I was firmly behind it and could use it as a shield in case she tried to karate chop me in the nuts. I survived. "Your turn," I said. I tell her it's been a good day on the markets and she says the café's had a good day too. She thinks I was a little harsh banning the fish pie lady. I cook something for us to eat and we eat it while watching the DVD.

8pm

Time for a little bit of research.

I check though ADVFN Toplists and see if I can find anything interesting. Look closely at some of the day's risers, chart breakouts and market maker buying. Have a close look at three shares, but though they look good, the market sizes are too small for my purposes. However, I like the look of finance company Cattles - it seems to be winning business, its last statement was excellent and the chart looks strong. It reports in three days though. I add it to my watchlist. Also add Homeserve. It provides all-in insurance for things like people's gas boilers. Looks a good business but the spread of the shares seems to be quite volatile - if I did buy I'd have to watch my timing. Have another look at Almusac but still not totally convinced - another one to watch and wait on.

9pm

The Dow closes 100 points down - that should mean the FTSE will open up around 20 points lower tomorrow. Check Cantor Index's website (a spread betting firm) and they are quoting tomorrow's Footsie to open down 25. That's fine as I'm still heavily into shorts.

9.10pm

Join Elizabeth to watch a recording of The Sopranos, our favourite show. Why can't our TV companies make a show as fine as this?

10pm

A final check on my emails. There's one from Norman, a regular correspondent who is disabled and often in pain. He seems to find my site a good diversion and he pretends to buy and sell my shares and tries to beat me to a good sell or buy. He chats about shares and the fact he's going to play Santa later this year. It's good to know I provide him with entertainment, it makes running my website worthwhile. One reader's just finished a good investment book he'd like to recommend to others. Another tells me he can get rice pudding at 21p a can. One reader thanks me for recommending a book called Investment Madness, and says it has stopped him over-trading. It's great fun getting emails and though I don't give advice I think my site does push people in the right direction.

10.30pm

Settle down to watch a new show on E4 called The Great Love Swindle. They filmed at the café last week and we're looking forward to seeing it on the TV!

11pm

Time for bed. Sometimes I dream about a share that's going down suddenly getting a bid approach and going up 30%. Sometimes I dream I'm a spy getting hunted by the bad guys. And the other dreams I'm keeping to myself!

Note: This was written before the birth of my son Christopher. As you can imagine things have changed a bit now! (i.e. what is sleeping and where do you find the time to do it?)

3

Is Trading Right For You?

Let's talk about you

First, the warning

Before I launch into my trading methods and how they have developed over time, I want you, dear reader, to examine why you want to buy and sell shares.

Obviously, you want to make money. Perhaps one day you see yourself in my position – in bed with your laptop trading shares and not having to go to work. But those little warnings in italics you'll see in most financial ads are spot on. You know the ones you have to take out a magnifying glass to read. The warnings are far too dull – I reckon something more suitable would be (in large letters):

The Naked Trader Approved Investment Warning

If you start buying shares or spread betting all gung-ho you will lose money. You'll put most of your cash into a penny share that people on bulletin boards tell you will be a ten bagger – and you will lose that money. Then you'll try to win back that money so you can just break even and stop. But you'll lose the money you put in to try and break even. Your missus will then find out, and will dump you. Your house will get repossessed and you'll find yourself inside William Hill putting your last tenner on a horse.

And that will lose too.

That might sound a bit far-fetched, but it *has* happened. A lot of people thought they'd make their millions, but actually really did lose their shirts – and their houses.

Many started trading during the late 90s when the tech boom was in full bloom. You might remember the bloke featured in *The Sunday Times* every week, who sold his house to raise money to trade? He gradually lost most of his capital and ended up having to go back to a day job.

There were plenty of sad stories on the financial bulletin boards: how traders were trying to hide huge losses from their wives and how it affected their lives. (You can read about some true disaster stories later in this book.)

It wasn't just would-be traders who lost a lot of money however, those who entrusted their money and portfolios to, what seemed like, very posh and upmarket brokers also lost huge slices of their wealth. Others used advisory brokers to run their ISAs and PEPs with mostly terrible results. A friend of my wife invested £25,000 with an advisory broker in 1999. The total left in 2003? Just £7,000. And she was told her portfolio was 'low risk'!

By the middle of 2000 reality dawned and shares tumbled. But, even then, most traders and investors simply held onto their shares. They just could not believe a company they'd bought into at, say, £14, was now only worth £1 a share a few months later. And many just kept on holding until these same shares were only worth a few pence.

For example, look at Marconi's share price between 2000 and 2005.

Marconi: September 2000 – September 2005

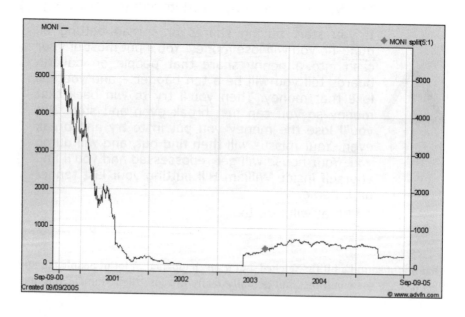

Why all the doom and gloom?

Why have I been reeling out these horror stories?

In a way, it's to put you off trading! "But, hang on, I've just paid good money to buy this book and now you're trying to put me off," you could rightly wail. However, I'm just trying to put you off going into trading for the wrong reasons and in the wrong way.

Don't think you'll get rich quick, it probably won't happen. But if you take things easy, be careful with the amount of money you put in and learn from your mistakes, then I am happy to encourage you.

If you're going to sell your house to raise money to trade shares, with the idea of becoming a millionaire in double quick time, then I strongly suggest you take this book back and get a refund.

[*Publisher's note*: We think The Naked Trader is just joking here.]

Can you afford to trade shares?

Before you buy a single share, I do urge you to look at your finances carefully and honestly. Ask yourself:

1. Where is the money coming from that I am going to use to trade?

2. Can I honestly and realistically afford to lose a lot of it?

It's unlikely you will lose the lot – if you are careful and follow the rules laid out in this book – but it's not impossible. It is quite possible that you could lose 20-30%, if the market runs against you for a while.

Maybe you have £10,000 spare sitting in a building society account not earning much interest. Will you feel OK about it if you end up with £6,000 after six months of trading?

- If the answer is "yes" to the above question, then go for it!

- If the loss of the money would devastate you, keep it in the nice safe account and maybe trade when you can afford to.

Perhaps you've suddenly come into money unexpectedly – say £50,000! Great – as you weren't expecting it and, presuming your financial status is OK, then no reason why you shouldn't invest £15,000 of it.

Are you a compulsive gambler?

Let's presume you have the money to play with. One final thing to check: are you a compulsive gambler?

- Do you bet on the horses, buy scratchcards, go to the casino, play online betting games on a regular basis? And does that give you a feeling of excitement?

- Do you feel unable to stop doing these things because they are really enjoyable, even if you are losing?

- Do you hide your bets from your partner?

If the answers to any of the above are yes, then give this book to someone else, HA! because you would be enabling your current addiction, and losses on the markets can be difficult to control.

Your temperament would also not be right for trading. You need to be cold and unemotional to trade, but you will feel the same 'rush' when buying a share as you would do backing a horse. So as an EastEnders' scriptwriter might say, "Leave it out!"

Blimey, after that lot I wonder whether I have any readers left!

Summary

Don't trade if:

- You can't afford to lose the money.
- Shares going down will make you miserable.
- You are likely to get emotionally involved.
- You have, or could have, a gambling problem.

4

Getting Started – The Trader's Toolkit

Introduction

You may already be trading shares: you have a broker and know how to trade shares using the internet, etc. If so, you can just skim the next few pages.

If though, you have never, or hardly ever, bought shares over the internet, then let's get started!

First, as any good scout knows, you need to be prepared. This includes having the following kit:

- a computer with internet access;

- an execution-only broker;

- real-time price feed; and

- a notebook and pen. Oh, and

- a cup of tea.

I'll go through setting up the above in the following pages. (Except the tea – come on I can't do everything for you.)

The toolkit

1. Computer and internet access

The computer's the easy bit. You've probably already got one, and it will almost certainly do. If you don't have a computer, then almost any new computer will be sufficient. You don't need the latest, most powerful computer to trade shares.

And as long as you have access to the internet that is reasonably efficient, that'll be fine.

A few tips:

- **Broadband is definitely best.** It will save you a lot of time and is worth the extra money.

- **Don't go for a laptop.** I find them too fiddly for trading purposes yet continue to use one. If you do get one, attach a keyboard and a mouse to it – much less fiddly.

- Do **use anti-virus software** on your computer.

- Do make sure you **backup your data.**

- In case your computer crashes, **do have a backup** system in place. This should include having to hand a printed record of your accounts and the telephone numbers of your broker.

- If you're using internet access at work, there may be a **firewall**, which could stop you accessing your account or real-time prices. Check and see. Perhaps you can persuade your boss to let you have access so you can do a bit of lunch time trading!

2. Opening a stock broking account

There are now countless ways to make money from trading without even having to open an account with a normal stock broker. There's spread betting, fixed-odds betting, CFDs, betting exchanges, options and futures. It's never been easier to play the markets. However, even with all these exciting-sounding ways of trading, I still believe new investors should start with a basic stock broking account.

It's the best way to start. Why? Because it's straightforward. And you can only lose whatever you put in (which is not the case with things like spread betting or CFDs).

Other accounts, such as spread betting, can be added fairly quickly once you've gained enough experience. I generally use a stock broking account and a spread betting account to do 95% of my trading. That's not to say the other methods do not have their merits, but I'll come to those later in the book.

Types of stock broker

How do you choose – there are so many brokers! Open an investment magazine, such as *Investors Chronicle*, and you'll see plenty of ads for stock brokers.

First, we need to distinguish the two types of stock broker:

1. *Advisory brokers*: these brokers will give you advice on what stocks to buy and sell, and even, if you want it, will trade on your behalf (this latter type are called *Discretionary brokers*).

2. *Execution-only brokers*: as the name suggests, no advice is given at all. You're on your own.

An advisory broker might at first seem the better choice, but these accounts are more expensive than the simple execution-only type, and the idea that brokers are experts, who actually know what stocks are going to rise, is so old-fashioned it seems quite quaint!

Anyway, as this book is about how to trade for yourself, you should be looking for an execution-only broker, rather than an advisory one. I'm sure the reason you bought this book was to make your own decisions. So, from now on, when talking of brokers, I am writing about execution-only ones.

Selecting a broker

It's difficult to recommend specific brokers as their services and charges are changing all the time. Also, different brokers are good for different people. For example, some people may value highly the charting service offered by a broker; whereas for other traders – perhaps with their own charting software – such a service is not so important. Some brokers are better for active traders than for longer-term investors and vice versa. However, I can give you a few pointers.

First, and probably most importantly, find out how much they charge per trade. I would estimate a current average charge of about £12.50 per trade.

- If a broker's charges are much **higher** than that, think about looking elsewhere.

- It is possible to get deals **lower** than that, but anything below a tenner – be a little careful, as they will need to make money out of you another way.

Charges can vary depending on how much you trade (the more you trade, the less the commission). Some brokers charge more for the first few trades a quarter then a bit less for the rest. All the charges and small print should be listed on the brokers' websites.

Note If you don't trade much you could be hit by an inactivity fee by your broker, so check that too.

But remember, as with every service in life, it doesn't always pay to take the lowest quote.

Each broker's service tends to be a bit different. For example, some brokers' websites may offer free charting facilities, or a news service. Other brokers may have a better relationships with market makers so can get you better buy and sell prices.

Most online brokers will be able to shave a small amount from the buy and sell price of a share for you automatically, though not in all cases. So, for example, if the price of a share you want to buy is showing at 100p – your order will probably go though at 99.8p or 99.9p. This is because the market makers all compete for business and so can offer slightly better prices to attract the business.

Of course, if you are not happy with the broker you choose, it's easy to switch. Alternatively you could split your initial stakes and use two brokers, and eventually switch to the one you prefer.

Broker checklist

A checklist when looking for a broker:

1. Check the broker's website.

   HSBC £11.95

   ↓

   £6.95.

2. Trades should cost no more than £12.50.

3. Watch out for hidden charges.

4. Use the bulletin boards to check up on what is being said about brokers – there is nothing like word of mouth.

5. Consider opening accounts with two brokers and compare their services directly.

6. Be prepared to shop around. There's very little reward for being a long-term, loyal client of an execution-only broker. Brokers are prepared to offer great deals to new accounts – exploit this!

Tip Personally, I mainly use Squaregain, E*Trade and Barclays. My website normally has a good offer from Squaregain – see www.nakedtrader.co.uk.

Below is a list of some of the top online brokers. Check through their sites and see what they have to offer you:

Reference – stock brokers

- Barclays Stockbrokers – www.stockbrokers.barclays.co.uk

- E*TRADE – www.etrade.co.uk

- Hargreaves Lansdown – www.h-l.co.uk

- myBroker – www.mybroker.co.uk

- self trade – www.selftrade.co.uk

- The Share Centre – www.share.co.uk

- Squaregain – www.squaregain.co.uk

- TD Waterhouse – www.tdwaterhouse.co.uk

Share certificates

Share certificates are a thing of the past – forget about them. Most online brokers use *nominee accounts*. This means you don't get a certificate, you are the electronic owner of the shares. Personally, I think it's great as:

- trading digitally, rather than with paper certificates, is usually cheaper;

- no more lost certificates; and

- settlement is much faster – once you sell a share you can re-invest the money right away.

Note For those of you reluctant to give up the smeared ink on dead trees, a digital-paper hybrid settlement does exist. For further information ask your broker about Sponsored Crest Membership.

---

3. Real-time prices

So, you've got a computer, internet access and you've signed up with an online broker. What next? Real-time prices are the next ingredient to add to your Trader's Toolkit.

Shares can move fast – so access to real-time prices is vital. The good news is that these days information – previously only on offer to professionals – is now easily available to all.

It *is* possible to get free real-time prices with some brokers, and this is something to assess when opening an account with one. However, I get my real-time prices from ADVFN.com because:

1. I simply prefer the ADVFN price service to that on offer from brokers; and

2. I feel more comfortable with the ability to check market prices from a source independent of the broker who actually transacts my orders.

I've used ADVFN since it launched and I find it provides me with all the tools I need to research my stocks with real-time prices too. The good news is that much of their service is free. Of course, you only get basic services for free. They also have quite a few premium services which, after a while, I would recommend you investigate. But, to kick off with, free is fine.

For the purposes of the book, I'm going to use ADVFN as the basic information supplier.

How to use ADVFN

Best place to start? I guess it's the home page and I'll assume you've already registered with ADVFN. (If you haven't registered yet, hurry up, we've got stocks to trade and money to make!)

ADVFN home page

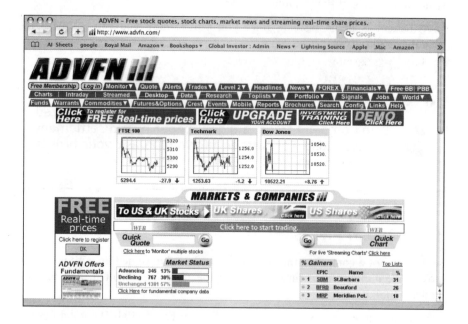

The main thing you need to focus on is the navigation menu near the top of the page (see the screenshot above). I'll go through the sections you need to be interested in initially.

1. **Monitor:** this is the most useful page! This is the basic list of shares that you are interested in and may want to follow on a day-to-day basis.

2. **Quote:** gets you a quote on the current price for any share.

3. **Trades:** data on buys and sells that have taken place in the share of your choice.

4. **News:** obvious...it's, er, financial news!

5. **Financials:** very important, has lots of info to help you research a share.

6. **Free BB and Premium BB:** these are the bulletin boards that investors use to gossip.

7. **Toplists**: one of my favourite pages. Contains rankings of stocks by all sorts of criteria, such as top movers of the day. Basically, a great place to find out where the action is happening.

The other buttons you'll want to use in time, but these should get you going.

Let's look at the information you get when you ask for a quote on a share.

Stock symbols

You'll quickly realise that everything on the ADVFN website (as with most other stock market websites) revolves around something called *stock symbols*. These are short (three or four character) symbols used to represent stocks listed on the London Stock Exchange.

The table below lists the symbols for the ten largest companies on the London Stock Exchange

Top ten largest companies on the London Stock Exchange

Company	Symbol
BP	BP.
HSBC Holdings	HSBA
Vodafone	VOD
GlaxoSmithKline	GSK
Royal Bank Of Scotland	RBS
AstraZeneca	AZN
Shell Transport and Trading	SHEL
Barclays	BARC
HBOS	HBOS
Lloyds TSB	LLOY

Note: Be careful, the code for BP is 'BP.' – including the stop.

These symbols are also – rather confusingly – sometimes called EPIC, or TIDM, codes. Throughout this book I'll refer to symbols, codes or EPICs interchangeably. (I hope you're not falling asleep at the back there – this is important stuff!)

If you don't know the symbol of the company you are interested in, you need to find out what it is. The best way to explain this is by way of an example. Bear with me, this is simple stuff...

Example: finding the right symbol for a stock

You've come across mention of a company called Broadcastle in the paper, and you want to find its current share price and start doing some research on the stock.

1. On the ADVFN website click the *Quote* button in the top menu bar.

2. If you knew the stock's symbol already, you could at this point simply input it into the box (to the right of where it says 'Symbol:'), click the OK button, and you'd be off. However, if you don't know the symbol, then type 'Broadcastle' in the box, and then click the 'Search' button.

3. A page should come up with, on the right hand side, a table with a title 'Search results'. Just one stock should be listed, which is the one you want. From here we can see that the symbol for Broadcastle is BCS.

4. At this point you can return to the main *Quote* page and input 'BCS' as the symbol (or ADVFN make it easy for us, as clicking on the symbol itself jumps straight to the relevant Quote page).

You'll see that there's quite a bit happening on the ADVFN Quote page. It's worth spending some time finding your way around this page. Included on this page:

- There's **price information** (such as last traded price, current bid and offer, the high and low prices for the day and the volume of shares bought or sold).

- There's also some summary **financial data**. (You can see at a glance the company nearly makes more than £3.8 million in profit a year and the market values it at £40 million.)

- The rest of the page shows you the **latest news** stories and the **chart**.

Using the ADVFN Monitor

You may decide you want to start watching Broadcastle regularly, so you should add it to your 'Monitor'. You'll be able to track its real-time buy and sell price, amounts traded, highs and lows of the day and whether there are any new news stories.

To start your 'watchlist' of shares, just click the 'Add Stock' button (near the top of the page).

You can add as many shares as you like to the Monitor. Remember, first find the code, then just add it to your Monitor.

You can have loads of different monitors. For example, you might want to track different types of shares. You could call one monitor 'FTSE 100' to keep an eye on the FTSE, and one called 'Small companies' to track the smaller sector.

ADVFN also has cracking research facilities too. I'll show you later how to use these to your best advantage.

Reference – real-time prices

ADVFN is not the only source for real-time prices, below are the main ones. It may be worth opening accounts with two or three real-time price companies in the event of your favourite breaking down.

 ADVFN – www.advfn.com

- Interactive Investor – www.iii.co.uk

- MoneyAM – www.moneyam.com

- Proquote – www.proquote.net

4. Notebook

So computer sorted? Broker account on the way? Access to real-time prices set up? A couple of shares in your monitor? Good, we're nearly there. Final thing, I also recommend keeping a notebook handy. It's always good to jot down ideas, share prices and bits of info.

Also try and be disciplined and keep a trading diary – write down everything you've bought and sold – the prices transacted and the reasons for buying or selling. This will come in handy later when you analyse why you made money, or lost it... It's possibly also worth buying a punchbag and some boxing gloves from your local leisure shop. Then, when you've lost money you have something on which to take out your frustration!

Your trading environment

Stay clutter free!

Keeping a clear head is very important when it comes to share trading. And it's just not possible if you're surrounded by clutter. I think it can seriously affect trading decisions if you're surrounded by hundreds of old fag butts, empty bags of crisps, loads of bits of paper, newspapers and empty beer cans. Clutter will subconsciously put you under more pressure when making trading decisions.

Therefore, keep a clear desk and a tidy office and your head will feel clear too. And this will help your trading. Tea and toast is also vitally important to good trading.

KISS – Keep It Simple Stupid

Don't make trading far too difficult for yourself. What I mean is, don't overburden yourself with dozens of trading screens plus a bank of TV screens in every corner of the room.

That's just to impress the girlfriend/wife/friends, right?

Keep it simple. You don't need to start buying chart systems and complicated software to start trading. All you need is access to news stories, fundamentals, charts and real-time prices. You can get this from free websites, or you might need to pay a small amount to access them. That's fine.

But don't go buying multi thousand pound systems if you're starting out. All they will do is confuse things. You need to keep that mind free to concentrate on just one thing: is that share a good buy or not? I promise you your expensive systems are just dumb computers. Stay with the simple stuff.

Anytime you catch yourself drooling over a glossy ad for a trading system promising to make you millions, walk away and just think of Baloo Bear from *The Jungle Book* – it's all about the bear necessities!

One day, when you've made your first million, by all means fill your office with impressive, flashing machines. But not for starters.

Final warning

I probably sound like an old fart warning you about this, that, and the other, but you are about to step into a world which is cut-throat. And I would really like you to make money.

It's very easy to get caught up and excited in this fast-moving world of shares, but don't just dive into everything you like the look of. Think carefully about the stocks you buy, and the prices you pay. If you miss a price, you miss it – like buses there's always another one coming – one of the golden rules of trading is not to chase prices if you miss a trade.

LIKELI
?
G

Before you make any real trades (if you've not traded before) I suggest you try paper trading first. Make a note of trades and track the profitability on paper, without making real transactions in the market. This, by itself, won't make you an expert trader. One of the major problems for traders is the mistakes they make when under pressure – which won't be felt when trades are only theoretical. However, paper trading can be useful at the beginning, when you're still learning your way around the jargon and technology.

And never just jump into a share because you're bored and want some action.

Right, lecture over!

5

What You Need To Know To Start Trading

Offer → buy
Bid → sell.

Introduction

In this chapter we're going to look at some of the 'voodoo' topics of the market.

1. Spreads

2. Trading costs

3. Normal market size

4. Trading hours

5. Why shares move up or down!

6. The trouble with market makers

7. Volumes

I'll accept that some of this may not be immediately fascinating, but they are essential to understand before making that first trade. This is because many new traders lose money in the market as they don't understand what's going on. So you've got to get your head around these things!

Spreads

Although you will often come across references to the 'share price', the idea of the price of a share is actually a little more complicated than it may seem, and people new to the market can get confused over this. First, we need to define some terms:

- *Bid price*: the price at which you can sell shares to the market.

- *Offer price*: the price at which you can buy shares from the market.

- *Spread*: the difference between the offer and bid price.

- *Mid price*: the price half way between the bid and offer prices.

- *As traded price*: the actual price at which the last trade took place (this might have been at the bid price, at the offer price, or anywhere in between).

Note

A key point we can see from the above is that – at any one time – the price for buying shares and selling shares is different.

Let's look at an example.

Example: bid-offer spread, Burren Energy

Screenshot of the bid-offer price of Burren Energy

Burren Energy(BUR) FREE reports								Click for Fundamentals	
Name	**Symbol**	**Market**		**Type**	**ISIN**			**Description**	
Burren Energy	LSE:BUR	London Stock Exchange		Equity	GB0033942946			ORD 20P	

	Change	**Change %**	**Cur**	**Bid**	**Offer**	**High**	**Low**	**Open**	**Volume**	**Chg Time**
↑	1.5	0.2%	717.5	717.5	719.0	717.5	712.356	712.356	18,079	08:56

Sector	**Turnover (m)**	**Profit (m)**	**EPS - Basic**	**PE ratio**	**Mkt Cap (m)**	**NMS**
Oil & Gas	87.102	48.478	28.4	-	997.2	15000

Type	**Size**	**Price**	**Tr.Time**	**Units**
O	1,000	717.81	08:55	GBX

Recent News				
Date	**Time**	**Source**	**Headline**	**More**
12/08/2005	13:54	AFXF	ROUNDUP Burren cuts stake in Congolese oil fields in 35 mln usd deal	
12/08/2005	08:42	AFXF	Burren sells part of Congo's Kouilou, M'Boundi stake for 35 mln usd UPDATE	
12/08/2005	07:59	AFXF	Burren Energy to sell 10 pct stake in Congo's Kouilou project for 35 mln usd	
12/08/2005	07:00	UKREG	Congo: Farm in by SNPC	
11/08/2005	08:03	AFXF	Burren Energy makes mandatory offer for 20 pct of shares in India's HOEC	
11/08/2005	07:00	UKREG	Launch of Open Offer in HOEC	
21/07/2005	11:36	UKREG	Drilling Update (Correction)	

In the above screenshot we can see that Burren Energy has a 'bid price' of 717.5 and an offer price of 719.0. That means, if you want to sell the stock you'll get 717.5p a share, and if you want to buy the stock you'll have to pay 719p.

Say you buy 20,000 shares at 719p, costing £143,800. If you changed your mind immediately after having bought the shares and wanted to sell them, you'd have to sell at 717.50. That's £143,500 so you are down £300 (before even taking into account the commission cost and stamp duty).

The *spread* is the difference between the offer and bid price and, as can be seen in the above example, is a real and significant cost of trading.

Tip Be aware of the importance of the spread, and realise that as soon as you buy a share, you're down on the deal.

Spread size

You'll soon find spreads can be wide or narrow.

Obviously the narrower the spread, the better for us. Spreads will be very narrow on heavily traded stocks like those in the FTSE 100, and wider on the smaller stocks. On some stocks, especially in the junior AIM market, spreads can be ridiculously wide.

For example:

- Look at the bid-offer spread for a **large company** like Vodafone. The bid-offer prices quoted could be 130-130.25. That's a spread of just a quarter point (approx. 0.2%) – it's tiny.

- But for a **small AIM stock** the bid-offer price could be 10-12. That's a spread of nearly 20%! If you bought at 12, the shares would have to go up 20% – just to break even!

Tip If I'm buying a smaller company, a spread of 5% is about as much as I'll allow. If the spread is more than that, I would seriously have to consider not buying, even if I like the look of the company.

Always work out what the percentage of the spread is. If you're rubbish at percentages, ADVFN will tell you the percentage under 'financials'.

Summary

- Remember: you're losing money as soon as you buy a share. + *STAMP DUTY*
- Work out the percentage of the spread. *TRANSACTION COST.*
- Be cautious about trading a share with a spread over 5%, and never + *SPREAD* over 10%.
- The wider the spread, the bigger the risk.

Trading costs

The costs of buying and selling shares can add up quickly, so here's a rough guide to possible costs.

They are generally three elements to share trading costs:

1. the **commission** charged by your broker *and*

2. (said through gritted teeth) a nasty and horrid tax on buying shares called **stamp duty**, *and*

3. the **bid-offer spread**.

Stamp duty is set at 0.5%. So if you buy £5,000 worth of a shares, the government will take £25. Of course this tax is outrageous. Why we should have to pay a tax to buy shares in companies I will never know. But there is no point bleating about it – we have to pay.

You only pay stamp duty on a buy, so when it comes to selling a share, it again is just the commission due to your broker.

So, let's take an example of a buy and a sell and how much it costs.

Example

You buy 1,000 shares in a company at 500p. Total value: £5,000.

Costs:

- Broker commission: £12.50 (average)
- Stamp duty: £25

Having bought the shares, you decide to sell them immediately, but because of the bid-offer spread, you may only be able to sell them at 495p. Total value: £4,950.

Costs:

- Broker commission: £12.50 (average)

(Stamp duty only applies on buys.)

So:

- Total direct costs (commission + stamp duty): £50
- Indirect cost (a result of the spread): £50

Beginner investors sometimes forget to factor in the cost of the spread, but this is a real cost. So, direct costs of £50 are bad enough. Factor in the spread, and total costs might be around £100! That's 2% of the trade value gone just in costs. Put another way, the share price has to rise 2% just to cover costs.

This is in the age of the internet, discount brokerages and efficient trading platforms. Imagine what it was like before, when broker commissions were a cool £50 or more!

So as you see, the more you trade the more the costs will stack up. In the above example, trade 5 times, and you've knocked up total costs of £500. I probably pay around £3,000 a year to trade.

It means if your mind is set on say becoming a day trader – that is buying and selling a share on the same day for a profit – you have to be really good to cover the costs, and that's one of the reasons 99% of would-be day traders fail.

Normal market size

Listen up at the back: don't be tempted to skip this bit because 'normal market size' sounds boring and you feel it's time to shut the book and watch some TV. Stay with me – this is important and easy to understand!

It's important because you can rule out buying some shares you like the look of, just because of the share's normal market size.

You may think you could buy as many shares as you like in any company, but it doesn't always work like that. It might be true for FTSE 100 stocks, but one has to be very careful when buying a smaller company.

Normal market size (usually abbreviated to NMS) is the number of shares market makers guarantee to sell or buy at quoted prices. If you want to buy or sell shares in a quantity above the NMS it can lead to problems.

NB : NEW STUFF !

Let's look at an example.

Example: normal market size, Leeds Group

Screenshot of the bid-offer price of Leeds Group

Leeds Group(LDSG)								Click for Fundamentals

Name	Symbol	Market		Type	ISIN	Description
Leeds Group	LSE:LDSG	London Stock Exchange		Equity	GB0005100606	ORD 12P

Change	Change %	Cur	Bid	Offer	High	Low	Open	Volume	Chg Time
0.0	0.0%	14.0	13.0	15.0	14.0	14.0	14.0		07:40

Sector	Turnover (m)	Profit (m)	EPS - Basic	PE ratio	Mkt Cap (m)	NMS
Specialty & Other Finance	16.514	-1.632	-6.2	-	5.1	1000

Type	Size	Price	Tr. Time	Units
O				GBX

Recent News				
Date	Time	Source	Headline	More
04/07/2005	11:05	UKREG	Transaction in Own Shares	
22/06/2005	11:42	UKREG	Transaction in Own Shares	
10/06/2005	15:40	UKREG	Transaction in Own Shares	
27/05/2005	07:30	UKREG	Interim Results	
28/04/2005	16:02	UKREG	Holding(s) in Company	
21/03/2005	12:35	UKREG	AGM Statement	
07/03/2005	12:51	UKREG	Director Shareholding	

In the screenshot above we can see that ADVFN quotes the NMS of Leeds Group as 1,000 shares. That means that the bid-offer prices quoted 13-15, are 'good' only for trades up to 1,000 shares. If you wanted to buy, say, 8,000 shares the market maker may quote a higher price (than 15). Conversely, if you wanted to sell 8,000 shares, the market maker may quote a lower price (than 13).

But 1,000 shares at the offer price of 15p is only £150 – this is not a lot of money. You don't have to be a multi-zillion pound hedge fund trader to be affected by this.

If you wanted to buy £5,000 worth of Leeds shares (when its NMS is only £150), you could end up paying more than the current offer price of 15p. And when it comes to sell, you might have to accept a price below the prevailing bid price to get rid of them (or sell your holding in batches of £150, and incur multiple commission charges).

In practice, you can usually deal in two or three times over the NMS, or sometimes more, without being charged extra on the share quote. But you can't bank on it.

So, taking into account the NMS and the spread on Leeds, this share cries out: 'Don't touch me with a bargepole!'

Dealing in quantities larger than the NMS can result in being charged more than the share price quoted in the market. This means the share could end up being more expensive than the quote

> **Note** Dealing in quantities over the NMS also means that if the share price collapses you could be left with shares that are difficult to sell quickly.

suggests. What's worse is you may not be able to sell all your shares in one go, thus paying a lot more in commission costs.

So I am very careful and make sure the shares I buy have a decent NMS. I usually ensure the NMS is at least £2,000 worth of shares – though I prefer £4,000. To work out the NMS in pounds, simply multiply the NMS by the share price.

Summary

- Always check the NMS of a share before buying.
- You may pay more to deal in quantities larger than the NMS.
- Don't deal in shares with an NMS equivalent to less than £2,000.

Trading hours

The table below gives the daily timetable for the UK market.

Timetable of UK trading day

07.00	Regulatory News Services open
07.50-08.00	Pre-market auction
08.00	UK market and FTSE 100 Index Futures open
08.00-16.30	Continuous trading
14.30	US markets open
16.30-16.35	Post-market auction
17.30	FTSE 100 Index Futures close
18.30	Regulatory News Services close

Source: *The UK Trader's Bible*, published by Harriman House

For the moment, don't worry too much about the detail in the timetable, the main thing to note is that the UK stock market is open from 8am to 4.30pm, Monday to Friday.

> **Note** Don't try and deal outside these hours – it *is* possible to do this (e.g. via spread betting), but the spreads will be a whole lot wider.

And be careful of dealing in the bigger stocks between 8am and 9am – the spreads can be huge because there is no depth to the market and you could get caught out.

Why shares move up or down!

Before we go any further, I'd like to pause and answer a simple sounding question often asked by new investors:

"What makes shares move up or down?"

You might think that would be an easy question to answer. But the factors affecting shares prices are quite complex. I get emails all the time from investors very puzzled by the movements of shares. They get very frustrated, for example, when shares move and they can't see the reason why.

A classic example is when a share price falls following the release of good news (perhaps strong annual results). What a perverse market, people wail. But the explanation, for this case, can be found in the old stock market maxim:

"Buy on the rumour, sell on the news."

By the time the news is actually announced, all the information has *already* been assimilated into the price (i.e. look at the share price behaviour in the short period leading up to the announcement). When the news is actually announced, the smart money (having bought previously in the run-up) is looking to sell and bank their profits.

There are many reasons why a share might move. I'll examine some of the reasons in greater depth later. But for now, and to show how difficult it can be to know why your shares are doing well or badly, here are some of the reasons:

1. Broker upgrade/downgrade

Brokers regularly put out recommendations to their clients – the share may temporarily be affected by a buy or sell recommendation. You'll usually find your news feed will reveal which broker and what that recommendation is.

2. General market move

The whole market may move up or down – for whatever reason – and your share will move in line with the market.

3. Sector move

Say your favourite stock is a telecoms share. A different telecoms company may have put out a profit warning, so your share could be dragged down along with all telecoms stocks.

4. Institution move

An institution has bought or sold stock. (Big trades – such as those made by large institutions – are usually notified on the news wires one or two days after the event.)

⑤ Director buying/selling

Directors have bought or sold shares in their own company. Investors often follow movements by directors so more stock might be bought or sold than normal, moving the price.

⑥ Results/news story

If the price is moving quickly, check the news wire for any story. It could be a price-moving statement from the company or other news story.

⑦ Dividend dates

Look INTO!

The price will always move lower on 'ex-dividend' day. So if the dividend is 10p the share will move down around 10p.

? really? ALWAYS SPREAD BET THEN?

⑧ Tipped

The share has been tipped by a newspaper, magazine or one of the many tipsters.

⑨ Bulletin board manipulation

A tiny stock could soar because a group have got together to make it sound irresistible on the BBs. *DICKS!*

⑩ Market maker manipulation

Market makers are moving the price to encourage buyers or sellers to suit their own ends.

⑪ Surprise events

Something major happens like a terrorist strike – all shares could be hit. Or some political drama unfolds somewhere.

⑫ Rights issue

A company decides to raise money by offering more shares at a lower price. This usually lowers the price as more shares would be in issue.

⑬ Takeover/merger

Companies announce a takeover or merger.

My brief summary above shows just how on the ball you must be. Always know *why* a share you have a stake in is going up or down before taking any quick action.

CHECK NEWS etc... blah blah...

The trouble with market makers

The good

Market makers are charged with making two-way (bid and offer) prices for individual stocks. Without them, trading could be difficult in some stocks. For example, you might want to sell some shares in a company – but what happens if at that time there are no other investors wanting to buy your shares? You'd be stuck with the shares, as you couldn't sell them. Market makers are there to ensure that there is always a buyer, and a seller, for shares. In technical terms, they help create liquidity.

If you see a bid-offer price for a company at, say, 20-22p, it is likely those prices are being made by a market maker. The market maker is willing to buy shares at 20p from sellers, and to sell shares at 22p to investors wanting to buy. As an investor, you know that you can buy or sell shares in a company at any time – regardless of whether there are any other interested investors – because the market makers are in the market making a two-way price.

> **Note**
>
> When you buy, or sell, shares in the market, you are usually buying or selling those shares from a market maker – not transacting directly with other investors.

The difference in the buying and selling (bid and offer) prices is called spread (explained above), and it is the spread that provides the profit to market makers. To earn this profit, market makers have to abide by a number of rules set by the London Stock Exchange.

Because large companies (for example, those in the FTSE 100 Index) do not need market makers (i.e. there is never a shortage of investors buying and selling these stocks), it is only smaller shares – outside of the FTSE100 – that have markets makers. Any one company may have between two and fifteen market makers. The more market makers there are, the more competitive their prices have to be.

Market makers have to register with the London Stock Exchange to make a market in a specified company's shares. Once authorised, the market makers have to make *continuous* two-way prices – they can't just shut up shop when the market gets difficult for them.

So far, so good – market makers provide a valuable service to the market.

Or, perhaps not.

The bad

A quick glance at bulletin boards will reveal that market makers are not popular with traders.

According to some traders, they are the James Bond villain, the dalek and the bad guy with the moustache on Thunderbirds all rolled into one. Market makers decide the fate of your share and it's their to mess you about. They are your worst nightmare.

[handwritten: MA]

I think you get the general idea.

Why is this?

The reason is mainly due to the way they make their money, which can put them in opposition to traders.

Remember, market makers make their money from a share's spread. The more that traders buy and sell, the more money market makers make. Therefore, it is in the interests of market makers to move their prices around a bit to encourage active buying and selling of shares.

So, the market makers may move a price up to encourage you to sell your shares, or move it down to encourage you to buy. The result is that share prices can move in odd ways, sometimes with little seeming relation to the actual situation of the company.

This can be very confusing to new traders who see a price moving, but can't understand why it's moving. It drives a lot of investors crackers, especially if it makes you sell your share at the wrong time. Their sudden price drops or rises often leave me shouting words at my screen I'm sure my mother doesn't think I know.

Tree shaking

[handwritten: NEW STUFF ! I.E. DON'T PANIC ... CUECK NEWS BLAY!]

All sorts of 'tricks' are employed by the market makers. For example, when they drop a share for no reason, it's known by investors as a 'tree shake'.

One morning you'll roll out of bed, switch on your computer and see your favourite share is down 2p, then 3p, 5p and 6p...! You'll start to scream, sweat, swear and probably panic. Yes, that's exactly what they want you feel. In a panic, you'll sell immediately at any price because something terrible must be happening.

What's actually happening is that 'tree shake'.

It's designed to make you very afraid. Afraid enough to think the share's going down further so you should get out. Once you and a few others have sold out, the price will gradually start to go back up. This will also make you scream and sweat, and probably swear. At least the panic will have gone!

You've been shaken out! *[handwritten: GUTTED !]*

So why do they try and shake you out?

It may be because the market makers have a big buy order to fill, and they need your shares to fill it. Or perhaps the company is doing well, results are due and they want to get some cheap shares into their 'bank'. It's more likely they will get your shares by dropping the price, especially by doing it one pence at a time.

MAY WORK IN FAVOUR - BUY MORE?

 CAUTION

Tree shake antidote

Instead of panicking and swearing, here's what you do:

Check to see if there is anything on the news wires regarding the share. Then check if there is any major selling showing up. If there is no obvious reason for the fall, it's 90% certain that it's a tree shake.

So instead of selling, go and make a cup of tea and some toast and relax. Later in the day you can pat yourself on the back – you weren't shaken!

A tree shake will also usually only last a few hours. If the share continues to go down over a day or two it could be more than a shake. Watch volumes and see if there has been any serious selling.

A final point. If you do get shaken out of a share and it goes back up, sometimes it's best to swear a bit at the computer but then leave it alone. Otherwise you will go back in and immediately be emotionally involved with that share.

There is always another share, another day.

Large stocks

FTSE 100 stocks, and some other larger stocks, trade on what's known as SETS (Stock Exchange Trading Service). It's an electronic dealing system, where buyers are matched with sellers (and therefore market makers are not necessary). It ensures much tighter spreads. Prices are much less open to market maker manipulation.

If you see a large stock moving up and down quickly, you can forget about tree shakes, the share will be moved around more by weight of money.

There are also a number of stocks that have market makers and also electronic dealing called SETS/MM. So the share price can be pushed around by individuals as well as market makers. This is okay as it makes the spreads quite tight.

Just as this book is to be published, it looks likely SETS/MM will also be used for some of the smaller companies too. As I write I'm not sure of the effect this'll have, but I suspect I'll be discussing it on my website, www.nakedtrader.co.uk.

Market maker summary

So, markets makers: good or bad? Probably a bit of both.

There's no doubt that much blame heaped on them via bulletin boards comes from those who don't properly understand their role in the market (and it's not to help traders make money!) It has to be said that some criticism is just downright paranoid or a result of sour grapes.

But, on the other hand, market makers do play around with prices, which can catch unwary traders out. It's a fact of the market.

Generally, their influence is greater in smaller stocks, and this needs to be factored in when deciding what stocks to trade. At the end of the day, if you don't like the rules of the game, you should play a different game.

Volumes *BRING IT! LOL*

Trades – buys and sells

Volume is simply the amount of shares traded in a share. For example, if 109 million shares have been traded in Shell in one day (i.e. 109 million shares were sold and 109 million shares were bought – don't forget, they always have to match!), then we say that Shell's volume for the day was 109 million.

Why is it important? Because unusual volume activity with a share can indicate that something interesting is going on.

In addition, some data services designate trades made as 'buys' or 'sells' (depending on whether the trade price was close to the prevailing offer or bid price). It is then possible to calculate aggregate volumes for buy trades and sell trades.

Tip To access trade volumes, press 'trades' on ADVFN for the stock you are interested in. This gives you an up to the minute list of buys and sells going through.

I often get emails from confused investors who follow the volume of buying and selling in particular companies. Emails like: "Why is the share dropping when there are so many more buys than sells?"

Apart from market maker shenanigans that I've already discussed, this is because all the 'buys' and 'sells' you see listed on trade analysers are only *guesses* by a computer!

So when you see trades listed under 'buys' or 'sells', that 'buy' could easily have been a

> The lesson is to treat volume trade data with great caution.

GUESS?

'sell'! The trouble is, market makers can delay the publication of trades that are over the normal market size of a stock. So the trade you see at 14h20, could well have been made at 10h20.

The lesson is to treat volume trade data with great caution.

Trade codes

You'll notice that there is a letter which goes by every trade – that at least gives some sort of clue as to the sort of trade it is. Here's what the main ones mean.

T trades

This doesn't mean nice relaxed trades made over a cup of tea. 'T' by a trade, in market jargon, means 'single protected transaction'. The trade you see going through is someone who has bought or sold a lot of shares over a period of time and it all goes through as if it was one transaction.

That makes it hard to know whether the trade is a buy or a sell. But, as a general rule, if the share is rising it's probably a buy and if falling it's probably a sell. Quite why the buyers need protection I'm not sure!

X trades

When you see 'X' by a transaction, even if it's for a big amount of shares, you can kind of ignore it. This is just a parcel of shares being swapped between two parties. One wants the shares the other doesn't. So there are no real conclusions to be drawn and the share price is rarely affected.

O trades

'O' means it's an ordinary trade. This is normally broadcast immediately, unless it is over six times NMS in which case it can be delayed.

L trades

'L' means a late reported trade.

M trades

'M' is a deal between two market makers. Usually means one of the market makers is short of stock.

AT trades

'AT' is an automated trade dealt through the order book.

Really all these codes do is give you a clue as to whether a trade is a buy or a sell. The 'T' trade is the most important one to look for.

Things To Think About Before Buying

Develop a money strategy

Before you gallop into the world of share trading, it really is sensible to develop a strategy regarding what you expect back from the market.

However gung-ho you are, you are not going to double your money overnight. Set yourself a realistic target. Decide why you are going into the market:

- Are you looking to build wealth over a long period?

- Just want a bit of fun? (and that's all us girls wanna do!)

- Make a bit extra to buy a new car?

- Hoping it will help pay school fees for your kids?

- Provide a better retirement?

Think about what you want from the market, because what you want (and how much you want it) will affect how you trade.

Age matters

Much depends on how old you are and what sort of commitments you have. Here are some age groupings, yes, I know they are a bit stereotyped, but I guess you see what I'm driving at...

Age group: 20s

You have nice paying job and plenty of disposable income.

You might say: I want to get 50% *20%* back on my money and I don't care if I lose it; I have no commitments yet and I'd rather try and use money to make money than buy a flash car.

And that's fine. Go for some risk and it might pay off! Just don't kid yourself that you can afford to lose the money easily if you can't.

Age group: 30s

You have a wife and kids, a mortgage and commitments, but a little disposable income.

You may decide you want to take a few risks, after all you're on a good wage. However, you may want to keep a good proportion of your money in lower-risk stocks.

> However gung-ho you are, you are not going to double your money overnight!

Age group: 40s-50s

Your income may begin to fall and you have more commitments. So a low risk growth strategy might be best.

Age group: over 60s

Dividend and high-yielding shares may be of more interest now. Low risk is a priority as you may not be able to afford to lose any capital.

New investors

There are various types of new investors. For example, you may suddenly find you have £10,000 spare – now you feel is the time to stick it in the market. You could be thinking: I want to double or nothing – stick the whole lot in a couple of risky shares in the hope they double. Judging by the internet bulletin boards, that's what a lot of people do – and probably end up with £4,000!

So have a good think about your current status, and decide, at the very least, a general strategy. What exactly do you want, sonny Jim?

My advice

You may wonder what I think you should do – but this is difficult to answer unless I know your individual circumstances very well.

However, as a start, my favourite strategy would be to kick off with a £7,000 self-select ISA and try and grow it by more than you'd get in a building society – you might surprise yourself and grow it by a lot more! More on this strategy later.

Preserve your capital!

> **Note**
>
> Whatever your eventual strategy, bear one thing in mind: try and preserve your capital!

Preserving your capital is best achieved by keeping a close eye on any losses and cutting them (more on this later). Many of the best traders have more losing trades than winning trades! However, the money they lose on the bad trades is small, while the profits on the good trades outweigh the losses.

Remember, if you lose 50% of your capital, you will need a 100% gain just to get back to your starting position. And a 100% gain is asking a lot.

How much time do you have?

"Time is an illusion, lunchtime doubly so."

The Hitchhiker's Guide to the Galaxy

Remember the markets are only open during normal office working hours (8am-4.30pm). When you trade, you'll have to find a way to trade during these times.

> I don't believe you need to sit in front of the trading screen all day. About an hour a day is enough for most.

If you don't have access to the internet for at least a few minutes between these times on most days, give this book to a friend! Forget about the market and buy some premium bonds instead. (PS If you win the million remember your old pal Robbie.)

The more time you have to keep an eye on your investments, the better. If you work in an office and can keep an eye on your shares during the day that's a bonus. But you can still make money even if you are out a lot.

I don't believe you need to sit in front of the trading screen all day. About an hour a day is enough for most.

But that hour is crucial. Every day the market acts differently, and you'll get more of a feel for what's happening as you get more experienced. You could possibly even buy shares before you leave for work, check them at lunchtime and when you get home.

Evenings and weekends, when the market is shut, is the best time for researching stocks and re-appraising the stocks you have.

Market psychology – cutting losers, running winners

I've always had trouble spelling 'psykology'. But that doesn't matter as I have a very good editor who will make sure psy.. psc.., whatever, will be spelt correctly!

Market psychology is an important topic.

Because however cool you think you are, your buy and sell decisions will end up being affected by your emotions. And, being humans, we are very emotional animals. We let emotions rule various aspects of our lives (which often can be fun); and it's just the same with investing (which is usually disastrous).

Emotions, quite simply, get in the way of making good investment decisions.

So, imagine you're Mr Spock.... Be logical, Captain.

Emotions lead to taking quick profits…

We all want to feel good about ourselves, and selling for a quick profit makes us feel *very* good. The trouble is, our feel good emotions harm long-term investment gains because it stops us sticking with the winners.

Many investors even take profits if a share has only gone up 2 or 3 per cent. That's because they can proudly boast to themselves and others; "I banked a profit."

Not

… and hanging onto losers

Of course emotion is the main reason for hanging on to losers for far too long.

We hate feelings of regret, and selling a losing share makes us regret and maybe feel a bit mad at ourselves. We want to avoid that. So we'd rather watch the shares continue to decline, than take the loss and feel bad about it. It's stupid really, because eventually, when we sell even lower we feel even worse!

No!

Revenge on the market

There's another psychological problem when it comes to selling at a loss: feelings of revenge! We want to get our money back and that causes us to be emotional and start taking too many risks. If we've lost half our money we might be tempted to go for a small stock we think might double to get the money back – or some other dodgy trading behaviour.

This is where the unemotional stop loss (discussed shortly) comes into its own. That way a stock is sold without bringing in the emotions of regret and getting even. And that means you are less likely to make an overly-risky next trade.

On man and egos Loose it!

One of the main reasons investors lose money in the markets is their inability to sell something at a loss. This is mainly due to ego. Taking a loss is actually very difficult to do – especially for blokes – and I still find it difficult.

> You have to go against human nature when you take a loss, but you must steel yourself to do it otherwise you will not end up a successful trader.

Taking a loss means accepting you have got it wrong. If we just stick with the share, we believe it'll go back up, we might even make a profit and – hey presto – we were right all along. But usually the opposite is the case – the share keeps sinking and we lose more money. And absolutely every investor has done this and you will do it too!

A good example is when I bought Coffee Republic (see the 'My biggest disaster' page). When I bought the shares for 28p, if I had set a stop loss of 22p, and acted on it, I would have sold without emotion at 22p and lost only £500. As it was, with no stop loss, I eventually lost £7,000.

> Perhaps this sums it up well: experienced traders have a saying, "You have to love to take losses and hate to take gains".

Luckily for me, Coffee Republic was a bit of an aberration and now, well, 95% of the time anyway, I manage to stick to stop losses and use them.

Fortunately, things are better online. It was always difficult to phone a dealer and admit – to a real person – you'd made a loss and were now taking it. Whereas it's much easier to take a loss online (the computer isn't thinking, "what a plonker"!).

You have to go against human nature when you take a loss, but you must steel yourself to do it otherwise you will not end up as a successful trader.

Let's look at an example.

You want to buy a new share but you have to sell a current one to raise the cash. The choice for selling is between two shares:

1. Stock A is showing a loss of 20%

2. Stock B is showing a gain of 20%

Which share should be sold?

I would bet that, nine times out of ten, the investor would sell the stock that has gone up 20%, rather than sell the loser.

That's because selling the winner shows what a good decision it was to buy it and validates that decision. There's also an element of pride involved and it feels good to lock in the profit. It affects all us. Personally, I feel pretty good when I lock in a profit and extremely irritated when I have to take a loss!

You can also tell your best friend: "I just made 20% profit" – while you keep the loser to yourself! Bad move, buster, guess who's going to have to buy all the drinks tonight – do'h!

You really have to learn not to postpone the feelings of regret. Avoidance of regret is one of the main reasons investors lose money.

Perhaps this sums it up well: experienced traders have a saying, "You have to love to take losses and hate to take gains".

To a beginner investor, that will sound odd and counter-intuitive. And until he understands that saying, he will remain a beginner investor.

Setting targets and stop losses

As well as asking yourself what you want to achieve from the stock market, you need to decide what you want from every share you buy.

You should decide what you are trying to gain from buying it. Yes, I realise you are trying to gain money! What I mean is:

1. what sort of share is it;
2. what is the downside risk of the share;
3. what time span you expect to hold it; and
4. how much do you expect to gain?

5. Before you buy a share set yourself a target, and a stop loss.

And write them down!

(And not on the back of the *Daily Mail* that'll get thrown away in a minute – get a notebook!)

Your target is a rough guide to when you expect to take profits and your stop loss is where you should cut your position without emotion. A stop loss is a point you should set when you buy a share where you would take losses if the share has fallen.

Why are they so important and why should you use them?

> **Note**
>
> One of the main reasons investors fail to grow their portfolios is NOT taking a loss when they should.

This was much in evidence during the tech boom.

Investors bought shares, saw them soar, then watched them decline. Instead of setting a stop loss point they let the shares, in some cases, become worthless and lost all their money, instead of just some.

If you stick to a stop loss system, your losses will generally be minimised.

> ★ ★ ★ **Naked Trader Very Important Advice** ★ ★ ★
>
> The hardest thing in the world to do is sell at a loss – but please do it. I promise you it is the best thing to do.

By the way, once you've sold at the stop loss you will feel very relieved that you are no longer holding onto a losing stock.

What level to set a stop loss?

So at which point should you set a stop loss?

A good place is at about 10-15% below the price you bought the shares at. This is because if your stock has gone down by that much already, there is probably something up. If there's been a profit warning, definitely get out.

So if you've bought a stock for say 100p, think about placing your stop loss at around the 85p-90p area.

Once you are more experienced, you might set a tighter stop loss, perhaps even at only 5%, because you have worked out that it is the best way to do it.

Trailing stop losses *[handwritten: ? MAYBE - KEEP TRACK - TIME !]*

Some investors then use what they call 'trailing stop losses'. That means as the share you've bought into rises, so does your stop loss.

Say you bought a share at 100p and set a stop loss of 90p. If the share goes to 120p, re-set your stop at 110p. If the share then dips to 110p, sell up and take the profit.

Example

1. A FTSE 100 stock – let's take BSkyB. It's currently 620p. As a Footsie stock it moves around a lot so I might take a short-term view. I only expect, at best, a short-term 10% gain so I'd set my target at 680p. I reckon the rot might set in if it fell below 600p, but maybe give it a little extra slack so let's set the stop loss at a tight 590p. Three weeks later if it's 592p and slipping fast – you have your cue to exit! Sell! But if it's 685p, great you've made the money you wanted, take profits!

2. A small stock. Let's say Retail Decisions. It's 18p. Remember only one or two points movement is a big percentage. I'd set a stop loss at around 15% or about 14p. Target? About the same – around 23p.

In the end it's down to experience – and trial and error. But better to set some targets than having no plan at all.

You'll see if you go to my website, www.nakedtrader.co.uk, that I have a list of my current positions. Every one has a stop loss and target. You need to ensure you have done this too.

Monitoring stop losses

Generally you have to look after stop losses yourself. You might have a friendly broker who will keep an eye on it for you, but with an internet account it is difficult for them to do, and the stop losses with ordinary share trading usually can't be guaranteed.

However you *can* have an automatic stop loss with a spread betting firm (see the spread betting chapter).

Note

One thing worth mentioning about stop losses is that once you are out of the share if something happens to make you regain your faith in it you can always buy it back!

Capital gains tax

There is a cost to share buying that's even more horrid than stamp duty: capital gains tax! Governments really don't like it when we are successful so to put a stop to you making too much money, you have to pay taxes on share trading profits.

For the tax year 2005-6, you are allowed to make up to £8,500 in profit – after that you have to pay tax.

When I say profit, that is the *net profit*: all the profits on shares sold minus all the losses on shares sold.

Of course, most new entrants to the market will be doing well to make £8,500 in a year, so maybe it's not something to worry about, but it could easily affect you in a bull market.

What's even worse is that it is very complex to work out what you owe the taxman. You *must* keep a record of all your transactions. Luckily you will find your friendly broker will have kept them all for you (and you should be able to access them on their website using the 'history' function).

Giving general tax advice is always difficult, because everyone's tax situation is different. However, some quick tips to bear in mind:

1. If you hold on to shares for a few years you may benefit from 'taper relief', where you pay a bit less tax.

2. AIM shares only attract a 10% tax rate.

3. You can offset profits in a current year by selling shares bought in previous years at a loss.

But as a rule of thumb, once you've made a profit of more than £8,500 per year – you face paying CGT.

Why you should use ISAs

There *is* a way to avoid tax. No, not sticking all your profits in cash and putting it under the mattress and hoping the taxman doesn't find it. It's called (now don't yawn when I say this word): ISA! (Snappy, huh? Stands for Individual Savings Account.)

I know, you've seen ISAs advertised in papers, and hardly anyone has any idea what the point of them is. Well, thanks to recent government action most of the tax benefits of ISAs have been wiped away, but the big benefit is that there is no capital gains tax to be paid. Currently, you're allowed to put £7,000 in an ISA every tax year.

You might well say: what's the point, you can only put a small amount in so surely capital gains tax will never be a problem?

Wrong!

I have saved thousands upon thousands of pounds in taxes, that I would otherwise have had to pay if I hadn't put all my share money into ISAs (and PEPs as they used to be called).

As the years go on, and you build your portfolios, the ISA tax advantage becomes more and more apparent.

Example

1. Let's say you have a few good years and build up £150,000 of capital inside your ISAs. All tax free. Now say you have a very good year and turn that £150,000 into £250,000. That's a profit of £100,000. Outside an ISA that profit could cost a huge £36,800 in capital gains tax.

2. Say you put in £7,000, and you strike lucky – you bought a penny share that trebled. You sell and you now have £21,000 – a profit of £14,000. Inside the ISA – no tax. Outside, your profit will be taxed at £2,400.

Nearly all brokers will manage a self-select ISA in conjunction with shares bought outside. It is worth checking to see if they make any standing charges to look after your ISA. Most do, expect to pay around £15 a quarter.

There is no maximum amount you can build in your ISA. One chap who writes for the *Financial Times* has managed to build his ISA fund to over £1 **million!**

Withdrawal from ISAs can be made anytime, but once cash is taken out, it cannot be replaced except with your annual allowance.

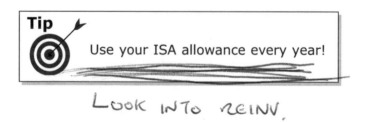

Tip

Use your ISA allowance every year!

LOOK INTO REINV.

Let's Get Trading

First things first

You're now set to deal, so, as Pink says, let's get this party started!

The big question is:

"Where do you start to find the right kind of shares to buy and sell?"

Which shares should you go for? And why?

Penny shares – newbies beware!

 Let me warn you straightaway: the first and biggest mistake made by new investors (known as 'newbies' on the bulletin boards) is buying tiny penny shares on a 'tip'. No!

It is *so* tempting to think about buying a share for, say, 2p, selling it for 4p and so doubling your money. Or, even better, buy at 1p, sell at 30p and become a penny share millionaire!

Nearly everyone does it when they start trading. I did it.

It really doesn't take much for new investors to be bamboozled into buying a tiny penny share.

You see a share that's 2p. You'll think... "Hmm, I could buy 100,000 shares for only 2p. That'll cost me two grand. If the shares go to 50p, I can make a profit of 50 grand just like that. Easy."

Believe me, it isn't going to happen.

The investment magazines don't help either. They often tip tiny shares. Also bulletin boards are full of other investors trying to tempt you to buy 'ten baggers' (shares that are forecast tol rise ten times in price).

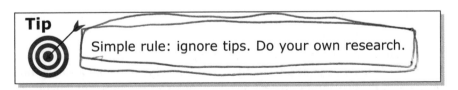

Tip

Simple rule: ignore tips. Do your own research.

It is so easy to get carried away. Remember the 90s tech boom? It was so exciting to buy a share in a new technology. How wonderful to buy shares in a company that's designed a new kind of speaker, some new plastic that will revolutionise catering, an exciting car gadget or an all-singing all-dancing mobile phone.

90% of the time these advances don't amount to much. The gadgets fail or don't work properly, or competition sets in quickly.

> **Note**
>
> Academic research shows that the real winners from new technology are consumers (who benefit from lower prices), and not investors in the company that invented or developed the product.

Take it easy and have a realistic target

What I'm saying is don't think 'exciting', especially in your first year of trading. Take it easy, and slowly. Think about companies that make money, pay dividends and have a solid business when you start to trade. After a while, when you are more experienced, maybe you can put a very small amount into a penny stock or a gadget company.

But, for now, your first target should simply be to make more money with your shares than you can in a building society. Say interest rates are around 5%. You have £10,000 that you can afford to lose to invest. You'd make around £500 over the course of a year if you stuck it away in a bank. Your initial aim should be to make a bit more than you'd get from a deposit account – say 8%, including any dividends received. If you make more than that, it's a big bonus!

That's all I made in my first year of trading. Nowadays I manage a lot more – usually between 25-45%.

It's all down to experience – I want to make sure you don't 'take a punt', lose some of your money and end up coming out of the market.

Listen to the Naked Trader – he knows of what he speaks (i.e. been there, done that). Now buy the T-shirt!

How do I find shares worth looking at?

Hey, stop asking me tough questions. Who do you think you are – Jeremy Paxman or something?

Oh, all right, if you insist. The best way to explain this is to tell you how I look for shares. Usually I try the kitchen first, then the living room but I usually find them under the bed. (You were talking about looking for shares, not looking for your keys, concentrate please – Ed.) GAYLORD!

My first stage is to simply try to find shares that *might* be of interest. I'm not saying I'll buy any of them rightaway – I'm on the hunt for shares I might buy soon, or I might buy next year.

Here's how I try to find shares at least worth adding to my daily watchlist.

Where I don't look for ideas

First, however, these are the places I *avoid* looking at to get ideas:

- Internet tipsters
- Bulletin boards
- Columns from 'gurus'

Where I look for ideas

These are my favourite places I look at for ideas:

- National newspaper round-ups
- Investment magazines
- ADVFN newswire
- ADVFN Toplists

Why do I use these particular sources?

Well, they have all served me well in the past and shares usually appear in these sources because there is a story to tell or the share is moving. Of course, if you read about a share rising in a paper or magazine it doesn't mean it'll carry on going up, it might well fall. But this is where I play detective and as they say 'do some research'.

Let's now look at these sources in more depth.

Newspapers

I usually get three national newspapers every day and have a good look at the financial pages. I'll look at any of the broadsheets including *The Times, The Daily Telegraph, The Guardian, The Independent,* and sometimes *The Daily Mail.*

The tabloids aren't much use when it comes to shares. In fact, one sign of the top of a bull market is when the tabloids start getting interested in the stock market. In other words, when the tabloids increase their coverage of the stock market, that's the time to get out of the market!

It might sound strange, but I don't bother with *The Financial Times* – I find it too dry and too heavy-going. It's more of an international, business-oriented paper. What I might buy is the weekend edition of the *FT* which has some thoughtful coverage of shares.

Within the newspapers, I take a look at the daily stock market round up – reporting on the shares that have gone up or down and why. I also have a scan of the news stories.

Once or twice a week I'll see something that looks interesting. I'll make a note of the share and why it might be one to buy.

Investment magazines

There are two main ones:

1. ***Shares Magazine*** · Check subscription £

    Appears to be aimed at the younger, more 'boys toys' readership. It has a number of strengths including a columnist who sifts through charts. There are also useful regular features on trading. I've spoken to the editor who I feel is pretty tuned in.

    (Published: Thursdays.)

2. ***Investors Chronicle*** – Check subscription £

    Investors Chronicle is a little more sober, and has a bigger circulation – its been around for a long time. It has some good analysis of company results, some good trading input and some interesting in depth pullouts which are well worth reading.

    (Published: Fridays.)

I think both magazines do an excellent job, especially as they have low circulations and therefore fairly low budgets. So I do rate both magazines as worth a buy.

But I would never be tempted to buy into the tips of either magazine (especially as these would already have been marked up by market makers on the morning of publication). You should look at the comments made by the magazines as a guideline and not just buy something because a company is recommended.

Sometimes a story about a company they write about might intrigue me, so I'll have a look at it. I especially like the round-up both mags do of recent company results statements. It's interesting to read their comments, they get some comments right and some wrong. Occasionally I'll notice a company I hadn't spotted before and pop it in my notebook to look at in detail.

A word of warning though – don't get fooled by the magazines which claim they produce winning tips. Some of their tips will turn out to be stinkers! Also, note that judging the performance of tips is not always straightforward:

- Was broker's commission and stamp duty taken into account?

- Was it actually possible to deal in the market at the prices used in the calculation?

- Often the aggregate tips performance will be heavily influenced by the stellar performance of one flukey share – if you'd missed buying that one share, the aggregate performance of the remaining tips might be nowhere near as good.

However, it is important to know which shares are being tipped (even through you don't buy them). This is because tipped shares will often increase in price before the market opens, and it's important to know why they rose (i.e. they were up on a tip). Otherwise you might buy them thinking there was more to the rise than just a tip!

A Genuine Naked Trader Tip

So my tip is: by all means buy these good quality magazines, but use them for reference and as prompts for trading ideas, not as a source of sure-fire tips.

ADVFN newswire

ADVFN has a 'streaming' (i.e. it continually refreshes itself, without having to reload the page) newswire – I tend to keep it running in the background. It covers pretty much everything that's happening. It includes company statements, directors' dealings, market reports, all you need!

Most company reports are published between 7am and 8am so I usually pay more attention to it early on.

Again, sometimes I'll find a company worth looking at, especially if a company report looks very positive. I make a note of anything that takes my eye from a company reporting to directors' buying – often waiting till the evening to check out the company concerned.

There are plenty of other newswires and websites out there too if you are interested in following the latest news.

ADVFN Toplists

These lists are a great way to look out for shares on the move.

The lists are compiled by a computer which has been given certain criteria.

ADVFN Toplists

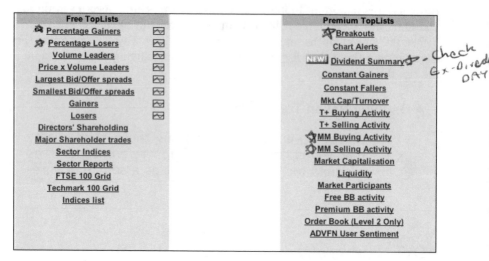

As you can see on the left are the lists you can have for free and on the right 'premium' that cost a fiver a month. That's a fiver put to bloody good use I reckon. For the fiver you also get access to the premium bulletin board where serious investors discuss shares and where my bulletin board is.

[Check my website www.nakedtrader.co.uk as I may have an offer running which means it'll cost you less than a fiver to access.]

The lists I particularly like are:

Percentage gainers and losers

In other words: the biggest movers of the day. These lists give an excellent snapshot of what is moving.

To find out why the share is soaring up or plunging down, there is often an 'A' by the share. You can just click on that to find out why.

I'm interested in both shares going down and up – because the ones going down this year could be the recovery play of next year. And the ones going up could have a lot further to climb.

Breakouts

One of my favourite share finding methods. This lists the shares breaking out of previously established ranges. A breakout is often significant.

ADVFN allows you to search for 52 week, 12 week and 4 week breakouts. My preference is for 52 week breakouts. A 52 week upward breakout often means a share is about to rise steadily higher.

Here's an example of a good 'un I found in this way.

White Young Green

The company is White Young Green.

White Young Green: September 2000 – September 2005

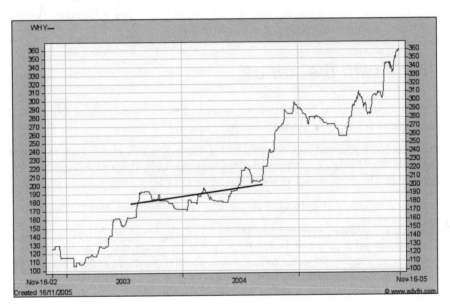

You can see from the chart that the share meandered between 180p and 200p for a whole year – anyone buying the share would have been stuck with a pretty boring investment!

One morning, the ADVFN Breakout list came up with *why* and the share had moved above 200p for the first time.

I quickly researched the share, liked what I saw, and bought in around 200p – it soon lifted to 220p. As I write, the share has soared to over 300p.

You can also search for 'breakdowns' – shares breaking down from previous ranges. This is a useful tool for looking for possible shorting candidates.

MM Buying Activity

A useful list for anyone looking for a short-term quick price in a share.

If market makers (MMs) are buying from other MMs it means they are short of shares and so the share concerned could bounce higher quickly.

If you're looking for a quick bounce, especially in the smaller shares, this is a very handy list. If you get in quick enough you could catch a good bounce. I've done this very occasionally – I usually research a share in the normal way.

I do use some of the other lists on ADVFN, but the ones above are my main hunting ground.

You, of course, should not necessarily copy what I do – you will end up finding your own methods of picking shares worth a look at.

Trade with the trends

'Let the trend be your friend' is a much quoted stock market cliché, but even if it's a cliché it's definitely worth remembering.

Sometimes, if you can ride the trend of a share you can make a decent profit out of it. So, if a share is gradually trending upwards, it may be worth joining the crowd. Or, if it's going down, it could equally be a good time to short it.

If only if it was as simple as that, we'd all be millionaires and no one would ever lose money.

The trouble with a trend is knowing when to jump off. That's really like anything in life. Flared jeans were a trend. So were platform shoes. So were the clothes I'm wearing now. But they went out of fashion. And the same thing can happen to shares – you've got to get out before the trend changes.

In 1999 the trend for tech shares was very much up. Buy any tech share and ride that upwards trend and you would have made serious money. But by early 2000, the trend ran out of steam and began to reverse quickly and sharply, leaving many investors out of pocket

Trend timing

So the trick is to try and spot the trend soon after it has started, and depart just before the trend changes and reverses.

That's a neat trick and I really wish I could pull it off every time! The fact is it is not possible to spot the start of a trend and the end of a trend. The secret is to try and ride at least part of the trend – not all of it. If you try to catch the exact the top and bottom, you'll come a cropper.

When Rothschild was asked how he got rich, he famously replied, "by buying too late, and selling too early". His message: don't try to time the top and bottoms of trends.

> **Note**
>
> What you must *not* do is try and fight a trend that's been established. Don't try and be clever and go against it.

Don't try and find the bottom or the top of a trend and call it before it happens. Be patient. Let the other chap grab a few of the points if you want, it doesn't matter.

So why does following a trend work?

Because as I've discussed already, man is a pack animal. And man (and the odd woman) tend to all pile into and out of shares at the same time.

Market traders find it hard to go with the trend because, naturally, traders are often mavericks and would rather be contrary. But over the long-term, I don't believe it's wise to fight the trends.

Next question:

"How do you spot a trend?"

You have to use a chart. Next topic...

Share charts and how to use them

Charts versus fundamentals

I think share charts are extremely important. In fact, some traders think share charts are so important, they trade only using charts.

A very good trader who I am friendly with believes share charts are like music. If you can read them and understand the patterns you will make money.

Personally, I wouldn't go that far. While I do believe in charts and use them, I don't believe you should trade shares only looking at the chart. There are so many other things to consider, especially what investors refer to as the 'fundamentals' – things such as company profit, loss, assets, etc.

Market commentators and tipsters tend to split into two camps:

1. **chartists** (also known as technical analysts); and

2. **fundamentalists.**

The chartists reckon they don't have to know anything about the company behind the share price. They don't care what the company does, what sector it's in, whether it makes profits or not, or when the next dividend is due. They believe the chart itself tells all and reveals whether the share should be bought or should be sold.

Are they right? Or are the fundamentalists likely to make more money?

I believe they both have some value and my method is to look carefully at both before buying a share.

Chartists have it both ways

I must admit to finding the chartists tricky characters. You can never really pin them down when it comes to giving recommendations. For example, fundamentalists might say a share was a buy because profits are likely to rise due to tightening control of costs.

Chartists, though, say things like: "The share looks a buy unless it goes to XX pence in which case it is a sell."

In other words, chartists tend to have 'get out' clauses with their recommendations, as it's next to impossible to measure their performance.

But let's look at charts for the moment.

Why charts work (to a certain extent)

A chart merely reveals what's happened to a share price in the past. But it does tell you what's very important: the price at which investors are likely to buy and the price at which they are likely to sell. What you have to do is try and spot where the trend is about to change.

Charts are useful for shares that are trading in a tight range. For example, a share price might move back and forth in the range 200-220p over a few months. You could try and play that trend: buy at 200p and sell at 220p.

Breakouts

Chartists get excited when the share price moves decisively out of this: by either falling below 200p (and staying below), or rising above 220p (and staying above).

Say the share had been going back and forth between 200p and 220p for a year – suddenly, it makes what is called a 'breakout'. It goes to 226p! That means it has broken out of a long-term range and is in a new, or breakout, trend.

That is one of the most powerful buy signals and that's the kind of chart signal that would tempt me in.

That breakout means it's quite likely the share will go higher – quite often simply because loads of investors spot the same event and all buy in together! The share could easily rise to 250p quite quickly riding the breakout trend.

But the share could easily rise to 250p, and then fall back to 225p – which would then become the new support level for the range. You really needed to have got out before the 250p level was reached and the share started to pull back.

Serco

Serco: September 2003 – September 2005

Here's a chart which is a good example of the above: the chart of Serco from September 2003 to September 2005.

As you can see, the share was stuck in a tight trading range around the 180p mark for quite a while, then all of a sudden...breakout! In February, the share rose out of its previous trading range and went all the way to over 220p in just over a month.

I spotted the breakout, but waited a bit for it to confirm and bought in at 190p. I also liked the company fundamentally – it was winning new contracts and profits were rising.

The trend started to reverse quickly in March – I saw the trend was breaking and banked profits at 218p. I then stayed patient and kept watching it.

It went down to 200p and climbed again. I bought in at 203p. I already knew the last time it went to 220p, so I was fairly confident it would do the same again. And it did!

A month later it was back up to 220p and it stayed there for a bit. I waited to see if it could break through 220p and, no, it started to retrace again, so I took profits.

In May, it went down to just under 200p again – now this had proved the bottom level of the share once already so I bought at 197p. And so it proved.

Once again, the share headed for 220p – this time I had no hesitation when it got to 220p and I sold again to bank more profits!

I hope you'll find that a useful example of using a trading range to your advantage.

Every little step I take

To keep you going during this ever so slightly more complicated part of the book hum the Bobby Brown song, *Every Little Step I Take* (or perhaps *Step on* by the Happy Mondays).

Shares never go up or down in a straight line, and generally move in steps. As discussed above, they tend to reach resistance points and rise and fall according to investor sentiment.

Vanco

Let's have a look at the chart of Vanco.

Vanco: September 2000 – September 2005

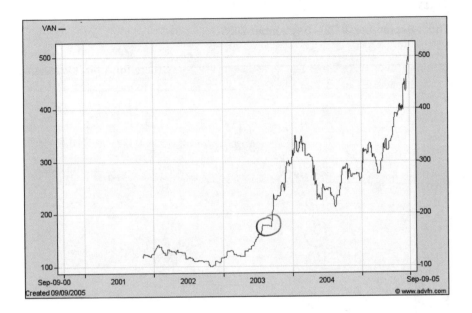

The chart quite clearly shows how this one has moved in well-defined 'steps'.

In 2003, you can see the share spent two months at 180p, treading water, but this can clearly be labelled a step.

1. In September/October of the same year the share moved up to the 240-260 level – oscillating between the two levels, thus creating another step.

2. In December another step is created at the 300p level. The final step is created in January at the 320p level, with a couple of attempts at 340p which fail quickly.

3. The share then retreats, but see how when it retreats it falls back down using the steps again.

   It falls back to the 300p area again before finally settling back at the 240-260p level.

Because the share settles for a while in this area, it is now fairly obvious what is going to happen next. The share will either start to aim higher and regain the 300p step, or a fall could see it retreating back to the 180p level.

So, all in all we have four very strong steps: 180p, 240p, 300p and 320p.

Any breakouts above or below these prices would see the next step or level reached again. A break again above 300p could see another attempt at the original 340p peak. A break above 340p would look even better and open up 400p as a target.

Thus

Thus: September 2002 – September 2005

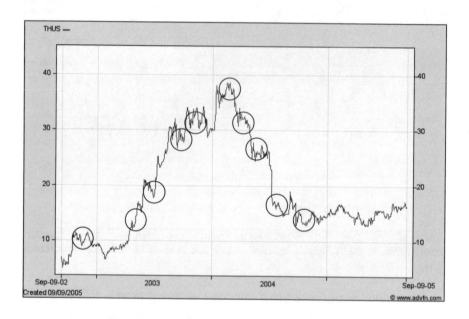

Another example is Thus – a favourite with smaller investors and me over the years. Pick this one at the right time and you can really make money. The chart really helps to show the steps.

A two year chart on this one shows its steps. These are at 10p, 14p, 19p, 28p, 32p and 38p. See when it falls, it falls down and rests on all the previous steps.

So it retreats from 38p back to 30-32p, then 28p and straight back down to 17-19p.

Again one can surmise here that a fall through 17p would see a slide back to the 14p area, whereas a break up could see 28p again.

Every time you look at a share you want to buy, see if you can see the steps over the last year or two. I find it makes it easier for me to decide whether or not to buy a share.

SIMILAR TO BREAKOUT (handwritten)

> **Note**
>
> One of the best signs is if it's just broken through the upside of a step, If you buy then, you could catch some upside, at least until the next step.

Patterns

You will very quickly come across charting jargon when you begin visiting bulletin boards – there are a lot of amateur chartists out there. I see no need, especially for new investors, to get bogged down in all the terminology.

You will hear things like: double tops, triple bottoms, big pants, MACD divergences and loads of other complicated patterns. (OK, I made up the big pants one.)

I'm not saying you shouldn't, at some point, learn about these and find out more, but for right now I think most newbie investors are better off using charts in a basic manner as I described in the last bit. See the chart as your chance to look at the history of a share easily and quickly note down the 'steps'.

I think it's far too easy to get bogged down in chartism – and many investors come a cropper when they rely on it. They read a few books about charting and then feel they are invincible! Of course what inevitably happens is the chart turns on them, and bites them on the bum. Which can be quite painful to you – and your bum. (Apologies to my mum who has got to this bit and is probably shocked I have said the word 'bum' three times.)

Head and shoulders

The one chart pattern, though that I think *is* worth getting to know is one which means 'avoid this share' – for now, anyway.

It is known as a 'head and shoulders' pattern (and we're not talking dandruff control shampoo here).

Big Food Group

Here's an example. Have a look at this chart of Big Food Group.

Big Food Group: September 2002 – September 2005

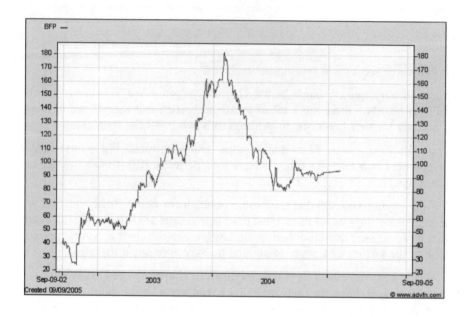

You should be able to see the 'head and shoulders' immediately. You see the head bang in the middle of this chart flanked by the shoulders.

What it means is the 'head' is where the share has made a new peak, and the shoulders is where it is falling away from the peak. It's generally a sign the share is overbought and is about to head downhill fast.

So while you're looking at the steps, it's worth checking to see there is no head and shoulders!

I could ramble on about charts for a bit longer but I think that's enough for now! But do research charts and decide for yourself whether to look at charts alone, or go fundamental or a mix of both.

Further reading

An excellent guide for beginners, and to help you get more advanced is *The Investor's Guide to Charting* (2nd edition) by Alistair Blair. This covers charting in depth, and if the subject interests you, this book covers most angles.

Get to know your area of expertise

There are so many shares out there, and so many different indices that you can trade. And you can trade them all in different ways. The whole array can be bewildering. Where to start?

What you must do is learn to specialise – don't spread yourself too thin. You're not Marmite. *Just in FTSE100.*

For example, I have a good record of picking shares, but for some reason I decided to have a go at trading indices. I suppose I wanted to try another area of the market to see if I could crack it. So I began to trade the FTSE 100 Index up and down.

I thought, "Well the Footsie is down 30 points I can't see it going any lower today so I'll bet on it to go up".

'Bet' being the operative word.

What I was really doing was a mix of gambling and boredom buying. I was just guessing, tossing a coin and hoping! This is no way to invest and I started losing money on this. I soon stopped!

Of course it would be a different matter if playing indices was my area of expertise and if I used some kind of skill to do it. But I didn't.

So while I suggest you gradually look at every area of the market, do be careful about launching yourself into a new arena without doing the proper research or knowing what you are doing.

If you are going to look at a new area, paper trade it for as long as possible until you are sure you know what you're doing.

8

Trading Secrets Revealed

How to research a share

My research involves finding out everything I can about a company before I consider buying in.

I look at everything I can, and much of the research involves trying to pick out the negative things – I guess I'm trying to put myself off! I use every scrap of info I have to come to a decision – and so should you.

Note

Good research means if you reach a decision to buy you really are sure it is worth buying into.

Don't skip the research

It's only human nature to try and skip doing a lot of research. After all, it can be pretty boring, and it's more exciting to just press the 'buy' button on a whim.

Much more fun to buy a penny share because a bulletin board punter has posted up some pretty charts and posted something about 'amazing news' on the way. Don't!

I urge you get down and dirty: do your research. Don't skip it and be serious about it. Find out anything you can, however you can. This is your money you're playing with and if you really want to make a profit there's no such thing as enough research.

And whatever you do, don't see a share and think "I fancy that one" then do research only looking at the positive stuff and ignoring the negative... that's not research! i.e. don't pretend to research because you're going to buy the share anyway.

There are many ways of researching a share and I'm going to share with you how I go through it.

When I find a share that interests me from the sources already mentioned, I find I can discount about half of them immediately, which is rather handy. This is because I subject each share to a quick but stern filtering process!

The Naked Trader Filter

Generally I will discard and not proceed further with any share that:

- is AIM or Ofex listed;

- is a loss-maker;

- has a big spread (more than 5%);

- has a small market size (i.e. small market cap.); or

- has the word 'challenging' in its last report.

These five filtering processes alone tends to get rid of a lot of them.

Why do I pick these five filters in particular?

Because I believe the criteria weeds out the high risk stocks.

I can easily check this criteria on the ADVFN quote page for the company concerned. All this info is under the 'financials' button for the company concerned. I check for the occurrence of 'challenging' under the news reports part of the quote page.

Dividend check

Next thing is to check dividend payouts.

If it doesn't pay a dividend, why not?

I wouldn't necessarily rule out a non-payer (like one of my favourite shares Vanco), but I'd find out why. If it's a fast-growing company like Vanco it may want to spend its money on growing rather than hand money to shareholders – that's okay.

- **Rising dividends** put a big tick in my book. I check these under the 'financials' button.

- If I see a **falling, or cut dividend**, I would probably end my research there – it's not a good sign.

Chart check

Next is a look at the chart for the last year – that's at the bottom of the quote page on ADVFN.

Is the line higher once it reaches the right-hand side, or lower than when it started? The former is a good sign as the share is in an uptrend. If it's lower, I'd have to look into it further but it puts it in dodgier territory.

I'd also take a look at the three year chart too.

Company background check

The next step is to find out what the company does and look back through the history of the last couple of year's news stories.

I like to see rising profits, turnover and a gradually improving share price. I look to see when it reports next. Is it next week or in three months? If it's next week, could there be a nasty shock on the way or will those already in the stock be ready to take profits?

Any director buys? Generally a good sign.

Any big share movements reported? Any institutional buys? I check all this out.

ADVFN makes it rather easy as you can click on all the news stories going back over a long time. And they include director buys, etc.

What I'm doing is trying to build a picture of the company concerned, and this is what you should be doing. Keep clicking, keep reading.

Just because you see one thing you like about a company, don't just buy it on an impulse.

Note

Don't ignore things you don't like the look of because you suddenly fancy buying it anyway. Stay cool and objective.

Check the company website

I always check the website of any company that I'm thinking about buying.

This might seem obvious but I bet most investors don't bother. A company's website can tell you an awful lot. It should also help you to confirm that you know exactly what the company does to make its money! By the time I've finished reading a site I try to make sure I can say what the company does in a sentence.

If the website is a bit crap, one has to wonder if the company is able to compete in the 21st century.

If the company uses the website to offer goods to the public, how good is the presentation? Would *you* consider buying goods from its website, and if not, why not? If the site doesn't tempt you to buy, it could have the same effect on others.

Look up the company concerned and its site on Google. Perhaps try putting in the company name and adding 'reviews'.

Are customers getting their goods on time or are they slagging off the company?

All bloody good research!

If the company doesn't use its website to sell, how does it treat its shareholders? Does it have a good news service and does it contain up-to-date news about the company? It ought to at least have a copy of its last financial report which you should be able to download. You should be able to send an email to the company as a shareholder.

Tip

Send an email stating you are a shareholder and you want to know the date of the next AGM.

See how long it takes them to reply, the quicker the better. If they don't reply, what does that say about how they feel about their shareholders.

The other reason for visiting the company's website is to give you extra research material. You may learn more about the company, which might entice you to buy even more shares!

Sectors

I always check to see what sector the share is in.

This is rather important. Is it in a depressed sector or a buoyant sector? For example, as I write in early 2005, the oil sector is hot and the telecoms sector is depressed. I'd obviously rather buy into the current buoyant sector.

The other reason to check the sector is to check the sector PE (that's the boring price-earnings ratio). Again you can find that on the ADVFN quote page. It's worth having a look to see if the PE is in the same ballpark as other companies in the same sector. If it isn't, it might be worth trying to find out why.

Go shopping!

Are you thinking about buying a retailer? If so, go forth and shop!

Get out on the high street and see how the retailer is doing. Go at a peak time, weekend and then also have a look off-peak. Be a bit cheeky (I've done this myself). Get chatting to the staff, ask them how busy it is and how well they're doing. Their answers could be quite illuminating!

You can start off by "how's business... you busy?". If the retailer you are in is quiet during a busy shopping day (like Saturday) then take heed. If it's busy and the tills are ringing merrily, it could be a buy signal. Watch out for too much discounting though – if the tills are ringing but the totals going in are low, maybe the retailer is under margin pressure.

> # Note
>
> Retailers are one of the easiest sectors to research.

All you have to do is wander up the high street and check out what's going on. Of course the Christmas period is the one that really matters to many retailers. They do a fair percentage of their sales in the run-up to the big day.

Those who get it right will find their share prices rising come new year and those who get it wrong will be thrashed.

Ted Baker

Recently, the one retailer I bought was Ted Baker.

Ted Baker: September 2000 – September 2005

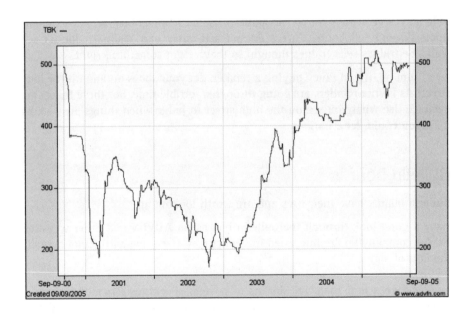

I did look at the chart and fundamentals, but I also loved the look of the branch and so did my wife Elizabeth. We could see people buying things and we bought too. In fact, as I write I'm wearing a Ted Baker shirt!

Ted Baker was a buy – I bought at 457.5p and it's been heading up every day since and sailed over 500p.

It seems to me retailers go in and out of fashion over the years – some have a 'buzz' and some don't. Ted Baker really has got the buzz. Its shops look great, the products are excellent quality and it's slowly opening more stores here and abroad.

Above all the wife gives it the thumbs up!

If you're a bloke it's certainly worth asking the girls where the hot place is to shop. If you mention a retailer and they start to frown, don't buy the shares!

For example, (although less clothes related) **WHSmith** – what a disaster some of the branches I've been into are. It's in a right mess as I write. They are going to put Costa Coffee in some of the branches, big mistake, I reckon – they should concentrate on their core products. A turn-off as a share buy.

Matalan I had a look at, but they were trying to flog Xmas cards for the dog or cat in your life. Honestly!

Brown and Jackson stores looked an interesting recovery play, and I visited a couple of their newer stores. I've been in and out a few times, but the process of changing its stores seems a slow one – I keep them on my watchlist for signs of improvement.

Side note: I've always found the names of some retailers bizarre. For example, Boots doesn't sell boots, Currys doesn't sell curry and Walmart doesn't sell walls. Selfridges sells fridges though, so they've got something right.

So to sum up, if you fancy buying a retailer, get your shoes on and hit the high street! As I write retailers are going through a terrible time, but these things are cyclical. Use what you see on the high street to judge when things are picking up – you could get a bargain.

Bulletin boards

Bulletin boards have their uses and are worth looking at.

Have a good look through the bulletin boards on ADVFN and other websites, for the company you're interested in. Sometimes a very busy BB is not actually the best of signs.

- A **bad sign** is if there are dozens of posters all enthusiastically discussing every tiny movement of the share. Even worse if there are posters claiming it'll be a ten bagger and the like, or posters saying they've bought some and are going to buy more, etc. And worst of all is when there is loads of inside bitching and backbiting between posters!

- The **best sign** is a reasoned, quiet but informed BB. It means the share concerned is actually more likely to be a winner.

What else to look for?

Sometimes you might find some handy research done for you. For example, if it's a retailer some posters may have visited stores and reported back their findings. Quite often with oil stocks in particular you can sometimes find very informed posters who know their way around oil exploration, digging for oil and the like.

Obviously, watch for the usual ramping as described later in the book.

Sometimes really good BB posters will make life really easy and will have cut and pasted in company statements and reports, dividend dates, etc.

However, don't take everything you read as accurate! Remember you are just using the BB to place another piece of the jigsaw.

All the news!

I click on pretty much all the news reports listed on ADVFN for the company, going back a fair way. These often include broker upgrades, directors' dealings and company announcements. This really is a must.

Also do a really good Google search. Put in the company's name and add 'news' or 'gossip' – you never know what it's going to throw up. There should be a few clippings from online newspapers and magazines.

Just see what you can pick up from a search. Reading news reports will give you a feeling for whether the company has a good or bad vibe.

Reading company reports

Every few months, companies have to put out a financial report. These sometimes come in the form of a full report which includes in-depth figures, and sometimes it's a trading statement which gives an indication of how things are going.

The statements are usually quite long and often complicated. And it doesn't seem to matter how badly the company concerned is doing – there will almost always be some kind of positive spin used on results. You really have to read through the positive spin and see if you can find the downside – more on that in a minute.

Now, I am no accountant and I'm sure you're not either. But there are one or two key things to watch for when reading a report.

Here's an example of a share I happened to research recently.

VP Group

It's called VP Group and it rents out specialist equipment.

Here's the beginning of the statement and it all looks good:

- Turnover up 11% to £83.5m (2003: £75.5m)

- Profit before tax up 19% to £8.9m (2003: £7.5m)

- Earnings per share increased by 18% to 14.59p (2003: 12.36p)

- Recommended final dividend of 3.4p per share (2003: 3.0p) giving a total dividend of 5.0p per share (2003: 4.5p) an increase of 11%

- Return on capital employed improved to 15.1% (2003: 14.4%)

- Net debt of £7.5m (2003: £6.1m), representing gearing of 14%, after

- Rental fleet investment of £10.8m (2003: £14.1m) and £6.5m of acquisitions during the year

---

That all appears good.

The figures are all rising well. The company has debt, but so do most companies and it's not much. It's bought other companies and made some investments.

I would now read the full report to try to find out what the company does, and how it makes its money.

I can see it has various different rental divisions. Reading it carefully I can see all the divisions are improving nicely, apart from one called Hire Station:

This result reflects a very disappointing year for Hire Station, but one in which I believe we have started to lay the foundations for the future. As reported in my interim results statement, a number of measures have been taken to restore this business to a more acceptable performance including the appointment in November 2003 of John Singleton as Managing Director. His new management team has launched a series of initiatives to reduce costs and deliver sales growth. These include the consolidation of three administrative centres into a single national accounting centre, rationalisation of the senior and middle management structures, refocusing of the sales effort and closure of a number of branches. These changes have reduced the overhead cost base and will give us a clearer emphasis on revenue and profit growth in the future.

I don't like to see the word 'disappointing' in a report. However the company clearly lays out what it is doing to improve the situation in this division.

'Rationalisation of structures' means it's cutting jobs in the pen pushing department. Bad for the pen pushers, good for the share price. I like the fact there's a new management team.

It seems likely this division will be firing soon and will add to the next profits.

Finally the all-important 'outlook':

Summary and outlook

Overall, the Group has delivered another very satisfactory performance with some excellent individual results. Hire Station has been a disappointment but we have taken robust steps which we believe will provide a sound platform for the future.

Our ambition remains to deliver sustainable profit growth whilst further improving return on capital employed and we believe that the constituent elements to achieve this are in place.

The Group's strong balance sheet and low gearing enables us to take advantage of growth opportunities as they arise, as has been clearly demonstrated by the successful expansion within Groundforce this year.

Again, that looks good to me. They're doing something about their one poorly-performing division, and I like the sound of 'delivering sustainable profit growth'.

So from this company report I would certainly research the company more and think about a possible share buy in the future.

I ended up buying VP at 128p and as I write it is over 200p.

Now if I read through a company report and I started scratching my head, not really understanding what I was reading, I would probably decide fairly quickly to leave that one alone.

The same applies if they start to use clever accounting terminology. So instead of a simple report you start seeing things like EBITA (earnings before interest, tax, depreciation and amortization). Yes, exactly!

In fact if something doesn't make sense or doesn't ring true, leave it! There are plenty more fish in the sea.

Watch out for 'challenging'

I have one key method though of working out whether the company I'm holding should be sold, or certainly not bought!

This method simply involves looking for one key word.

'CHALLENGING'

In my opinion this word means one thing: the company is probably in some kind of trouble!

Two other words to look for are 'difficult' and 'volatile'.

My simple method works rather well.

Examples

1. For example, in the statement produced by **Henlys** on December 12th 2003, the word 'challenge' or 'challenging' was there five times! The shares went up after the statement, but I would have sold – five challengings are more than enough for me. By January the shares tumbled 40% on a profit warning, and by June the company was delisted!

2. A statement from retailer **Jacques Vert** in July 2003 contained two challengings, two difficults and a volatile! By May 2004 the shares were down 30%.

Surprisingly, the word challenging is often used in the same sentence within what seems a positive paragraph.

Regent Inns

Take this from a statement put out by Regent Inns on September 3rd 2003.

> *"I am pleased to report on a strong financial performance from our branded operations during the year, despite the most challenging of conditions in our market place."*

I held Regent shares at that time and the moment I saw that statement my finger was on the sell button double quick!

The statement also contained other phrases such as:

"In such a challenging trading environment..."

And challenging then got replaced by "difficult trading environment"... twice!

Amazingly the shares rose after the report, because on initial reading it seemed positive.

But my system told me two challengings and two difficults meant exit time. Just as well. I sold my shares at 90p and by June 2004 they were down to 40p – down in value by more than half.

Take a good look at the shares you might own. Read the company's last report. If you see challenging or difficult, you know what to do!

Well, that's how to nix a company. But what are the positive things to look for in a report that might show the share is a buy?

Positive factors

There are a few things I like to see in a company statement.

Rising dividends

The first and most important thing is a dividend rise. And even better if the company has been raising dividends consistently. Rises generally show a company is performing well, there is cash coming in and there is confidence in the future.

The company statement will tell you the next dividend amount and the last dividend amount. Go to the 'financials' button on ADVFN to check previous years payments.

Rising profits, turnover and a positive 'outlook'

I also like to see rising profits, turnover and a positive 'outlook' towards the end of the statement.

Now, talking of looking out for certain key words in company reports...

Naked Trader Secret System 'Traffic Lights'

Now if you're a bit on the lazy side like me, perhaps reading every word in a report is all too much like hard work! So I thought to myself, could I develop a system which would scan reports quickly and point out the key words I discussed above. I think the answer is, yes.

I've only recently come up with this system, which in seconds can scan a company report and issue buy, sell or hold signals. So it's a bit rough, and I need to develop it some more, but I think it really does work. The feedback I've had from website readers indicates it really works rather well. Give it a try.

I call it my 'traffic lights' system: red for sell, amber for hold and green for buy! What its really done for me is make it very fast to tell from a results report or an AGM statement what the state of play is.

How does it work?

I use a neat tool which is available for use at ADVFN. The tool can be set up by clicking on 'News > News Phrases' from the top menu bar. This will bring up a page called 'highlighted news phrases'.

You can add any number of words or phrases and those will be highlighted down any text you want to read. You can also put the words in any colour you want.

"Well, it's not that exciting!" you may splutter. "What's the use of that?"

I think there are loads of uses, and I'm still working out all the potential ones as this tool has only just been launched by ADVFN as I write.

Here's what I do – and what you should do as well!

Naked Trader Traffic Lights System

- Put 'challenging' into the first box, in red.
- Then 'difficult' into the second in red.
- 'In line with expectations' into the third in yellow.
- 'Exceeding expectations' into the fourth in green.
- 'Positive' into the fifth in green.
- 'Favourable' into the sixth in green.
- 'Profit up' into the seventh in green.
- 'Excellent' into the eighth in green.

Now look at the last company report of all the companies you hold in your portfolio and you will see those phrases highlighted in the different colours.

Now it's really quite simple.

- Any company report that you see with lots of **red** is a probable sell or, at least, not a buy.
- Any with **yellow** a hold.
- Any with **green** are potential buys.

The more greens the more positive, the more reds the more negative.

Now you may scoff at what might seem an over simplistic idea. And, of course, my system is only the basis to start some more in-depth research.

But I don't think you can beat it for a quick judgement!

I'm not saying for a minute that you should buy every company which has loads of greens or sell every one that's red, but it should give you an instant 'flavour' of the report. As you get used to the system, you could add your own words or phrases.

I'm still working on some new ideas for using this tool and it will become invaluable. I suspect it would be quite handy at some stage to pick a whole bunch of words, and have those highlighted on a streaming news service.

But that's for the future, I'll work on it.

Recommended reading

For more detailed ways of reading company reports, I recommend *The Investor's Guide to Reading Company Reports* by David Leach. It's an excellent and easy read and points out the small things in company reports to watch for.

Ooh excitement – PE ratios, market caps, yippee!

PE ratios

Yes, I agree, PEs and all that. Sounds dull and I usually yawn and turn over the page of any magazine I'm reading which discusses PEs. Hey! Don't turn the page over.... Oooops, too late.

In fact, as I'm writing this I'm tempted to go off and have a cup of tea and watch Richard and Judy, because anything is more exciting than writing about a PE ratio! If the Jehovah's call round I might invite them in for a chat rather than discuss PEs.

...(slurp)...

OK, I'm back from my break, I can't put this off any longer.

What the hell is a PE ratio and why do people go on about them?

It means price-earnings ratio and it is calculated as the share price divided by the earnings per share.

There – that's not too bad, is it?

But forget about the formula, it's what it really means that's important. The PE ratio represents the number of years it will take for the earning of the company to cover the share price.

Interpreting PE ratios

Examples

1. Company A has a share price of 10p, and earnings per share of 2p. The PE ratio will therefore be 5 (10/2). So, with earnings of 2p, it would take 5 years for those earnings to cumulatively match the share price.

2. Company B has a share price of 90p, and earnings per share of 3p. The PE ratio will therefore be 30 (90/3). It would take 30 years, with earnings of 3p to cover the share price of 90p.

One can say that the investors in company B are more optimistic than those in company A. Company B investors are willing to wait 30 years (on current earnings) for the share price to be covered by the cumulative earnings. If they weren't confident, the investors would sell their shares, the share price would fall, and the PE ratio would therefore also fall.

By contrast, company A investors are not so confident. They're only willing to give the benefit of the doubt 5 years into the future, for earnings to cover the share price.

In general, high growth companies (e.g. tech stocks) tend to have high PE ratios; whereas low growth companies (e.g. utility companies) have low PEs.

If a company has a high PE ratio, then the investors have the bid share price up because they are bullish on the company and expect it to perform well.

You might think, therefore, it's better to invest in a high PE company because it could do really well.

Sadly it's not that simple.

The market could be overvaluing the high PE company and it could come down to earth with a bump.

Personally, I quite like lower PEs. That's because the market isn't expecting much, so if I think the company could beat expectations, the share price could soar. I like my PEs to be around 12-20.

A comparative measure

The main use of PEs, though, is not as an absolute measure. If a company has a PE, of say 20, it is difficult to say whether it is a buy or a sell. However, the power of PEs is when you use them to compare one company's share price with another.

For example, if company A has a share price of 400p, and company B has a share price of 14p, nothing can be said about their relative values. Is company B better value than company A? We don't know. However, if we know that company has a PE of 12, and company B a PE of 32, we *can* say that the market values company B more highly than it does company A.

Of course, it may be that company B deserves its high rating – it may be a great company, while company A is a dog. So, it's not very useful using PEs to compare very different companies.

It's main use is in comparing similar companies – for example, those in the same sector.

For example, if a retailing company has a PE of 15, while the average PE ratio of all companies in the retail sector is 20, one could say that the company is undervalued relative to the sector. There may be a very good reason for this. But if there isn't, then the company may merit further attention as a buy.

>
> ## Note
> Always check a company's PE ratio with that of its peers.

My view

Personally, I find PEs too abstract and only give them a passing glance.

A problem with PEs is that different publications differ on the PE. So the *FT* might quote a different one from ADVFN. This is because some use historical earnings, some use forward earnings... blah, blah. Quite honestly, the whole thing washes over me, which doesn't seem to matter as I still make money whatever!

Another way of approaching this is to look at a company market cap.

Market caps

The market cap (market capitalisation) is the market value of the company, calculated as

> number of shares in the company x share price

For example, if a company has a share price of 50p and it has 40 million share in issue, then its market cap would be £20 million. The idea is the market cap is around the price someone would have to pay for the company if they wanted to buy it.

>
> ## Note
> It's really important to know what the market cap is of the company you are buying into, and is one of the first things you should look at.
>
> You can easily find the market cap on ADVFN, as it's to the right of the quotes page.

From the definition of market cap, you can see that it rises and falls directly in line with the share price. For example, if the share price rises 30%, then the market cap will also increase 30%.

Examples

Here's a couple of contrasting examples. Two companies, both making (as I write) the exact same profits – around £4 million.

One, though, is valued at £26 million and the other at £126 million – despite the fact they make near identical profits.

- That's because the first company, **Carrs Milling Industries**, makes flour. It's a good steady business with some possible growth, but not exactly exciting. That's why it gets the low rating (i.e. a low PE).

- The second company, **Vanco**, is an IT company which provides network solutions for companies. It gets the high rating (high PE) because business is booming and it could easily win big lucrative contracts. Looking to the future, Vanco is more likely to make bigger profits than Carrs so the market feels Vanco is worth a lot more.

So, when you are thinking of buying a share you need to look at its market cap and profits and decide for yourself how much more room for growth there is. It's something you need to consider carefully before you buy a share that has a high market cap compared to profits.

Can it really produce the goods? If so, the shares could steam ahead.

Or should you stick with a more lowly–rated share like the food producer – safer but maybe with less exciting possibilities.

The choice is yours, don't look at me to decide for you!

I personally like to hold both kinds of companies – if you go for too many companies with high ratings your portfolio could become unbalanced.

Dividends

Dividends are cash that you receive, usually twice a year, from a company in which you've invested. Most decent shares pay dividends.

They may at first glance seem to be quite small amounts, but I can promise you, over the years they can add up to an awful lot of money. Some companies payout more in payments than you'd get in a building society. So not only are you getting a capital gain (as the share price increases), but interest too!

So how do you find out when the company is likely to send you some money, and how much will it be?

Best place to go is ADVFN, or one of the many other financial websites.

Example

Let's take one share for example – Fenner.

As usual click for a quote (code: FENR). Just click on 'financials' – if you scroll down a little you'll see the actual dividend yield, which in this case is 5.3%. This is what you'll pick up over a year holding the share.

5.3% isn't bad – so you could hold this share and pick up more in interest than you would currently from a bank (unless you're reading this in 2008, when who knows what might have happened to interest rates).

Now scroll down a little further and this is where it gets interesting.

Under 'dividends', you can see all the dividends that have been paid out over the years.

The top line shows the next dividend amount to be paid is 1.98p a share. So, if you have 5,000 Fenner shares you'll get paid £99. That's the interim, or smaller half-year dividend.

Look on the next line and you'll see the final dividend for 2003 was 3.85p, or worth £192.50p for your 5,000 shares.

So over the year, a 5,000 shareholder will have picked up £291.50 in dividends.

Ex-dates

Now a question that must be in the top ten questions I get asked about shares.

When do you have to be holding the share to get the dividend?

It's quite easy. It's called the 'ex-date' - you can see in the Fenner example the 'ex-date' is August 4th.

Note

It means on August 4th the share is trading 'ex' or without the dividend. So if you held the share up to and including the close of play on August 3rd you are entitled to the dividend.

If you buy the shares on August 4th you are *not* entitled to it.

'Record date' is August 6th – that's the date where they go through the share register and make a list of all holders entitled to the dividend – just ignore this date, it doesn't really matter. The 'ex' date is the big one.

And when do you actually get the readies?

That's under 'payment date' further along the line on ADVFN which in this case is September 6th.

Now, often new investors say to themselves:

> "Aha! I'll just buy Fenner late on August 3rd, and sell early on August the 4th, and pick up the dividend. Say I bought 20,000 shares I'd end up with a nice cheque for £500 and only hold the shares for five minutes!"

Nice try, clever dick! Don't you think the market has thought of this not-so-cunning ploy!

Well, it has – so there goes your nice little earner.

Sadly, what happens on 'ex' day is that the share price will usually start the day lower by the amount of dividend. So if you bought the day before 'ex', and sell the day after, what you make on the dividend payment, you'll lose in the fall in the share price.

Dividend payments are normally announced whenever a company makes its twice yearly results statement. You'll usually find a paragraph in the results which states the next ex and payout dates.

Note

You really ought to know the dates of ex-dividends on your shares.

For example, Fenner would fall 2p on the day it goes ex-dividend. If you weren't aware that was ex day, you might panic and sell because you thought the share was being sold off, or it had dropped through your stop loss.

So pay attention to these dates.

Recommended reading

Very occasionally the market does *not* adjust the share price immediately to reflect a dividend payment. The window of opportunity may only be a few minutes after the market opens on the ex date, so this is really only for active traders to exploit. If you want to read more about this I'd recommend *The UK Trader's Bible* by Dominic Connolly.

Timing of buys

Dividends are one of the first things I look for when buying a share, especially if the dividend is being raised over the years. It means the company concerned is a decent cash earner.

Shares without dividends should have 'caution' stamped all over them. Usually companies without dividends can't afford payouts, so you need to check carefully whether they will payout in the future. I *do* buy companies without dividends sometimes, as some companies don't payout because they are busy funding their growth.

I believe a good portfolio should be skewed towards having shares that pay dividends – perhaps at least 75% of shares should be payers. In the end, I tend to look on a dividend as a bit of a bonus, rather than the be-all and end-all of buying a share.

I like it best of all when I can buy into a share around 6-8 weeks before it is due to go 'ex-dividend'. Because if (as I hope) it goes up before it hits the ex date, I am getting capital growth plus the dividend too.

I'm not a great fan of buying shares directly after the go ex-dividend as I reckon over time it's better to collect the payouts. I certainly don't sell just before the ex-date.

One of the reasons I like buying 6-8 weeks before 'ex' is that fund managers often buy into shares at this time, and shares rise more often than not leading up to ex date.

I especially like shares that payout at something between 3% and 4%. That's because I know I'm pretty much getting back what I would have done from a bank. And secondly, the company isn't paying out too much! If a company was paying 7% or 8% it's unlikely to be a company that would greatly increase in capital value.

If a company suddenly announces it is 'omitting' a dividend, alarm bells should ring, and the shares should probably be sold immediately!

Tax

When you receive a dividend outside an ISA or SIPP, it's important to hang onto the slip that comes with it as that's for the taxman. If you are a higher-rate taxpayer you have to cough up tax on the difference between the basic rate and higher rate. You should keep the slips for tax purposes for six years anyhow to be on the safe side.

If you are taking dividends within an ISA or SIPP, the dividend amount is usually just added to your balance and you can use the cash to buy other shares.

Some investors prefer to re-invest the money from dividends back into the share concerned – that can be arranged with the relevant company, but I'm not a fan of that method unless you are an older, long-term income seeker.

Portfolio strategy

An interesting question is:

"Is it worth buying shares just for the dividends?"

It really depends on your market strategy:

- **Low risk investor**

  The answer is yes, if you are an older investor and are looking for very steady shares with good dividends. For example, utility companies payout big dividends, however their actual share prices don't move much, so you won't get quick capital growth. But say you're 60-years-old and want to grow a fund slowly but surely with minimum risk, you could just go for an income portfolio of high-yielding shares.

- **Medium risk investor**

  A medium risk investor might look on dividend as a bit of a bonus.

- **High risk investor**

  This investor doesn't care about dividends because he only wants big growth, and the kinds of shares he invests in generally don't pay dividends.

My view

My view is this: I see dividends as an excellent way of paying for all my costs.

For example, as I write, my pension fund shows costs of £2,700 but income from dividends stand at £3,300 (after nearly two years of running my fund).

>
> **Note**
> I think if you see your dividend income beating your costs, that's a good sign you are building an excellent portfolio.

It means you're buying some quality shares and not trading to excess and paying out too much in costs.

If costs greatly outweigh dividend income it means two things:

1. you could be **overtrading**; and/or

2. you are taking **too much risk**.

So keep a careful eye on costs versus dividend income – if you are near to a balance, or the income outweighs the costs, give yourself a pat on the back.

Dividend summary

- Know your 'ex-dividend' dates.

- Go for 3-4% yields.

- Good to buy 6-8 weeks before 'ex' date.

- Payouts match or exceed costs: good sign!

Timing

Comedians ought to make good share traders.

After all, often it's not just their material that makes them funny, it's all about the timing of delivery. If they rush a joke they won't get laughs and the same applies if they're too slow.

It's the same with shares.

Research is not just about finding out what a company does. It's all very well having researched a share and you feel everything is good with it and why not buy. But timing is everything in life, and it's the same with shares. It's pointless buying a good company if you're buying it during a general market slump, as the share will probably go down with the rest regardless of your careful research.

You have to time your entry and exit points with any share.

Just because the company is doing well doesn't necessarily mean the share price is going to go up. You could wake up one morning and see a great-looking statement from a company. The share price is going up and you think: with results like that this share is going to rocket!

Not necessarily. Suddenly, just after you've bought, the price starts to head south because many investors were in this one already and have now decided to take their profits and move on, leaving you holding the baby.

So how on earth do you get your timing right?

Patience

There is always going to be some luck involved, but the key word here is patience. If you see that great statement, add that share to your monitor and watch it like a hawk. Take a look at the share chart over the last three years and get a feel for its movements.

Watch how it moves up and down over the days and weeks.

And pounce when you feel the time is right!

Okay, the share might start going up and you end up missing the boat, but so what? There is always another day, another share. There is simply no substitute for experience in these matters, and as you learn to buy and sell shares you will gradually learn about timing.

Note If you are very new to trading, the best advice I can give you is: if it is obvious that your timing is wrong and the share starts to move against you – just get out.

Leave it on your monitor by all means and wait for a different entry point.

I'll give you an example of how a piece of experience led me to not buy a share I was interested in.

Patientline

The share, Patientline, looked good to me. I was about to buy at 132p when I noticed it had been tipped by an investment magazine, *Shares* magazine. Their tip of the week.

So what? You might ask.

One strange thing hit me: *the share had not risen.* Small shares always rise when tipped by *Shares* magazine. But not this time. The market makers know there will be plenty of demand, and there was. Yet the shares stayed level despite plenty of buying. The next day they even dropped a little.

"Very strange," I thought. "I just don't like the look of this, something is not right."

A week later, an institution dumped nine million shares and the stock fell to 112p!

Really, it's a matter of knowing your share.

If you follow certain shares, after a while you will get a feel for their movements, and good timing for share buys and sells often can come from a trader's gut instinct as well as use of charts and fundamentals.

You will find this starts to happen once you get more experienced.

Research

The best way to explain how I do my research is to give you an example of a share I bought after my research. So, a look at Fenner – a company I dealt with earlier regarding dividends.

I find out the code is 'FENR', and click 'Quote' on ADVFN. This is what comes up on my screen:

Screenshot of ADVFN Quote page for Fenner

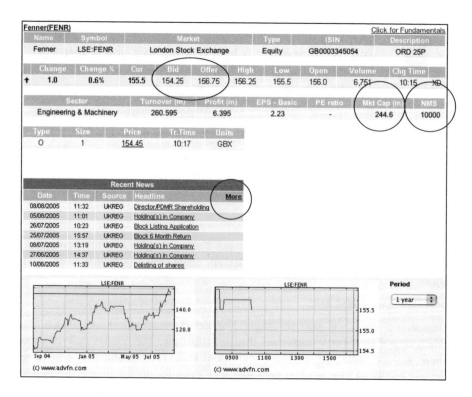

I can see the shares are 154.25p to sell and 156.75p to buy. So the **spread** is under 2% – good!

I can also tell a lot about the company with the other information on this quote page.

NMS is 10,000 shares – so easy to buy and sell a big amount. No problems there.

Market cap is £244.6 million, this means it's a small cap company but big enough to trade easily. At £244.6 million there is also plenty of room for the market cap to grow.

The next thing I look at is the **chart** – it doesn't take a genius to work out the company's share price has been going really well. You can see the last year's chart at the bottom of the ADVFN screen. I'd also take a look at the three year chart too. I can see from June 2003 to January 2004, the price grew from 70p to 100p. Then there was a plateau and then the share started to take off again.

The next stage is to discover why the price has been going up, and then try to see if there is a good chance the price could rise more. Certainly, looking at the chart, it appears there could be some way to go as the share is breaking out of a long-established range.

My next step is to look at the **news stories** from the last year or so. I need to find out what the company does, if its markets are expanding, what profits are like and if there's a dividend.

So I click on the 'more' button above the news stories to get all the stories from the past year or so, and I click on the last results statement to find out more.

Screenshot from ADVFN News page for Fenner

Date	Time	Source	Headline	Symbol	Company
19/04/2005	09:10	AFXF	Fenner H1 pretax 3.60 mln stg vs 1.60 mln	LSE:FENR	Fenner
19/04/2005	09:00	AFXF	Fenner in 54.1 mln stg fundraising, 44.6 mln stg bid for Wellington UPDATE	LSE:FENR	Fenner
19/04/2005	08:07	AFXF	Fenner in 54.1 mln stg fundraising to pay for 44.6 mln stg bid for Wellington	LSE:FENR	Fenner
19/04/2005	07:15	UKREG	Placing and Open Offer	LSE:FENR	Fenner Plc
19/04/2005	07:01	UKREG	Interim Results	LSE:FENR	Fenner Plc
27/01/2005	08:34	AFXF	UK smallcap opening - Fenner up on bid speculation	LSE:FENR	Fenner
12/01/2005	10:50	AFXF	Fenner says outlook remains unchanged for improved H1 result	LSE:FENR	Fenner
12/01/2005	10:30	UKREG	AGM Statement	LSE:FENR	Fenner Plc
20/12/2004	11:54	UKREG	Director Shareholding	LSE:FENR	Fenner Plc
20/12/2004	09:38	UKREG	Doc re. Annual Report	LSE:FENR	Fenner Plc
16/11/2004	12:30	UKREG	Blocklisting Application	LSE:FENR	Fenner Plc
15/11/2004	15:37	UKREG	Blocklisting Interim Review	LSE:FENR	Fenner Plc
10/11/2004	09:35	AFXF	Fenner FY underlying profit rises after strong H2 - UPDATE	LSE:FENR	Fenner
10/11/2004	09:32	AFXF	Fenner FY underlying profit rises after strong H2 - UPDATE	LSE:FENR	Fenner
10/11/2004	08:37	AFXF	Fenner FY pretax profit 6.39 mln stg vs loss 5.17 mln	LSE:FENR	Fenner
10/11/2004	08:02	AFXF	Fenner underlying profit rises after strong H2	LSE:FENR	Fenner
10/11/2004	07:01	UKREG	Final Results	LSE:FENR	Fenner Plc
28/10/2004	15:57	UKREG	Holding(s) in Company	LSE:FENR	Fenner Plc
25/10/2004	10:26	UKREG	Holding(s) in Company	LSE:FENR	Fenner Plc
22/10/2004	12:41	AFXF	Fenner sees higher annual oper profits: to maintain total dividend	LSE:FENR	Fenner
22/10/2004	12:03	UKREG	Trading Update	LSE:FENR	Fenner Plc
21/10/2004	11:25	UKREG	Holding(s) in Company	LSE:FENR	Fenner Plc
12/10/2004	14:36	UKREG	Notice of Results	LSE:FENR	Fenner Plc
07/09/2004	11:27	UKREG	Holding(s) in Company	LSE:FENR	Fenner Plc
30/06/2004	14:12	UKREG	Holding(s) in Company	LSE:FENR	Fenner Plc

Screenshot of ADVFN Results page for Fenner

```
                          Fenner PLC

                      2004 Interim Results

              "Recovery in first-half trading results"

    Fenner PLC, the global engineer specialising in reinforced polymer technology,
    today announces its interim results for the half-year ended 29 February 2004.

    Fenner is the world leader in the global conveyor belting market and its
    products include light and heavyweight conveyor belting for the mining and power
    generation markets, precision motion control products for the computer, copier
    and mechanical equipment markets, and specialist hose for the off road and
    commercial vehicle markets.
```

First, my usual look to see if the word '**challenging**' is in there: no!

Next, what does the company do?

Hmm. I like the 'world leader' bit, but my knowledge of conveyor belts is limited to cuddly toys on *The Generation Game*.

Next step is a look at the report summary:

Screenshot of ADVFN Results Summary page for Fenner

```
* The recovery in first half trading results indicated at the close of
  last year has been achieved
    - Our precision polymer businesses have performed well
    - Southern Hemisphere and China have enjoyed buoyant trading conditions
    - A slow start in the North American belting operations has been followed by a
      significant increase in order flow
    - Europe is experiencing a recovery in heavyweight belting volumes
    - Overall generally strong demand throughout our mining businesses
* Recent #4.7 million (net of expenses) capital raising has further
  enabled the expansion of the precision polymer business through the Indico
  (Europe) Ltd acquisition and the commissioning of the silicone hose plant in
  China
* Turnover increased by 6% to #120.8m (2003: #114.5m)
* Operating profit before goodwill amortisation and exceptional items up
  67% to #5.5m (2003: #3.3m)
* Profit before tax was #1.6m (2003: loss before tax of #3.3m)
* Earnings per share before goodwill amortisation & exceptional items
  increased to 2.27p per share (2003: 0.70p per share)
* Interim dividend maintained at 1.975p per share
```

Well, although I know nothing about heavy machinery and conveyor belts, I now have a rough idea what they do!

So, this looks a decent turnaround story. Plenty of stuff I like the look of here, such as: 'buoyant trading', and 'significant increase in order flow'. The company has shifted into a profit of £1.6 million after making a loss of £3.3 million.

Next move is to click on the ADVFN 'financials' button to have a look at the dividend payout.

And there is a decent looking dividend – nearly 6%, according to ADVFN – that's a good payout.

It's always worth looking at the 'outlook' part of the last report.

Screenshot of ADVFN Results Outlook page for Fenner

```
Outlook:

Commenting on the outlook Colin Cooke, Chairman, said:
"Heavyweight belting operations in North America are currently experiencing
stronger order flows which provide confidence for the remainder of the current
year.

"Continued and improved profitability is anticipated from South Africa,
Australia and China as these territories continue to participate in the recovery
and growth opportunities presented by their markets.

"The precision polymer operations are experiencing signs of stronger order
levels. This recovery, combined with volume increases from gains in market
share, will produce a satisfactory second half performance.

"Whilst the vagaries of exchange rate volatility remain difficult to predict,
we
remain cautiously optimistic for a satisfactory outturn for the full year."
```

Not bad. The only thing I'm not sure about is the exchange rate bit, and the 'cautiously' part of the optimistic.

However, on balance I still like the look of it as a whole.

I bought Fenner at 86p and ended up selling at a great profit at 128p.

New issues

New shares used to launch on the stock market all the time in the heady days of the crazy tech boom. Of course, since 2000 the new issues market has been much quieter, although recently many resource (mining and exploration) stocks have been listing.

I always look at all new issues coming onto the market, as I find there are gems that can prove eventual long-term winners. The one really good thing about *main market* new issues is they are reasonably safe investments.

They are, these days, 'priced to go' – meaning the price is set low to attract investors. So if you buy into a new issue, it's unlikely the share will go down much.

First though: how do you keep track of what's coming onto the market and what's just been launched?

My favourite way is to look at the *Investors Chronicle*, which features regular updates on all new issues, usually towards the back of the magazine.

Investors Chronicle new issues page

Future flotations

RED ROCK RESOURCES
Minerals

LIKELY MARKET	AIM
TRADING EXPECTED	29 JULY
LIKELY METHOD OF ISSUE	PLACING
LIKELY VALUE	£2.9M

Red Rock is a mineral exploration and development outfit.

Contact: ARM Corporate Finance
(020 7512 0191)

UBET2WIN
Gaming company

LIKELY MARKET	AIM
TRADING EXPECTED	26 JULY
LIKELY METHOD OF ISSUE	PUBLIC OFFER
LIKELY VALUE	£5M

ubet2win operates betting outlets located at seven racecourses in the UK and 11 in Ireland. An online gaming business is also planned.

Contact: Midas Investment Management
(0870 121 1445)

ARIANA RESOURCES
Mineral exploration

LIKELY MARKET	AIM
TRADING EXPECTED	26 JULY
LIKELY METHOD OF ISSUE	PLACING
LIKELY VALUE	TBA

Ariana Resources is focused on exploring for and acquiring gold and other mineral deposits in Turkey.

Contact: Ambrian Partners
(020 7776 6410)

D PHARM
Israeli biotech

LIKELY MARKET	AIM
TRADING EXPECTED	25 JULY
LIKELY METHOD OF ISSUE	PLACING
LIKELY VALUE	£15M

Chaired by former SmithKline Beecham boss Jan Leschly, D Pharm is a speciality pharmaceutical company involved in designing and developing new drugs.

Contact: Seymour Pierce
(020 7107 8000)

LATITUDE RESOURCES
Copper miner

LIKELY MARKET	AIM
TRADING EXPECTED	22 JULY
LIKELY METHOD OF ISSUE	PLACING
LIKELY VALUE	£14M

Latitude currently trades on Ofex and runs mining projects in the Chilean coastal range.

Contact: Collins Stewart
(020 7523 8000)

ENOVA SYSTEMS
Hybrid electric vehicles systems

LIKELY MARKET	AIM
TRADING EXPECTED	22 JULY
LIKELY METHOD OF ISSUE	PLACING
LIKELY VALUE	£20.5M

Enova's main focus is on the development of propulsion power management systems for hybrid electric vehicles – in particular buses, lorries and other heavy-duty vehicles.

Contact: Investec Securities
(020 7597 5000)

OXONICA
Nanotechnology

LIKELY MARKET	AIM
TRADING EXPECTED	20 JULY
LIKELY METHOD OF ISSUE	PLACING
LIKELY VALUE	£40M

Oxonica is a nanotechnology company with a focus on applications in the energy, healthcare and materials sectors and for products such as sun-care and anti-ageing treatments.

Contact: Panmure Gordon (UK)
(020 7459 3600)

URANIUM MINING CORP
Mining

LIKELY MARKET	AIM
TRADING EXPECTED	20 JULY
LIKELY METHOD OF ISSUE	PLACING
LIKELY VALUE	TBA

Uranium Mining Corp is involved in uranium exploration.

Contact: Nabarro Wells
(020 7710 7400)

RHM
Food group

LIKELY MARKET	MAIN
TRADING EXPECTED	19 JULY
LIKELY METHOD OF ISSUE	PLACING
LIKELY VALUE	£875M–£975M

As well as Hovis, RHM owns many of Britain's best-loved brands, including Paxo stuffings, Mr Kipling cakes and Bisto gravy.

Contact: Credit Suisse First Boston
(020 7888 8888)

ICVIEW See 8 Jul, page 8.

LAMONT PROPERTY
Commercial property

LIKELY MARKET	AIM
TRADING EXPECTED	19 JULY
LIKELY METHOD OF ISSUE	PLACING
LIKELY VALUE	TBA

Lamont Property was established to invest in commercial property.

Contact: WH Ireland
(020 7397 3000)

CONCEPT
Manufacturing consultancy

LIKELY MARKET	AIM
TRADING EXPECTED	19 JULY
LIKELY METHOD OF ISSUE	PLACING
LIKELY VALUE	TBA

Concept is a design and manufacturing consultancy business to the transport industry.

Contact: Collins Stewart
(020 7523 8000)

JARLWAY
Chinese concrete pumps

LIKELY MARKET	AIM
TRADING EXPECTED	18 JULY
LIKELY METHOD OF ISSUE	PLACING
LIKELY VALUE	£7.3M

Jarlway is among the biggest concrete pump makers in China, with its products used in construction projects throughout the country.

Contact: Hichens Harrison & Co
(020 7588 5171)

Source: Investors Chronicle

As you can see, it tells you the likely market, what the company does, its probable market cap, etc.

Note

I immediately ignore any companies that are to be launched on the junior market, AIM. I concentrate on those launching on the main market only.

That's not to say some AIM new issues don't soar in value; I have bought into the odd AIM new issue. But for newer investors I do recommend sticking to the less risky full listings.

In the two weeks before coming onto the market, a likely initial price range is suggested. It then depends on the state of the market as to what price the share is launched at. These days they are more likely to be priced at the lower end of a suggested range.

Furthermore, generally, only institutions get their hands on the shares before they launch.

New issues are much harder to weigh up than companies that have been on the market for a long time. For example, you can't simply scroll through recent news stories on ADVFN and do research in the normal way.

Here are the kinds of things I do to investigate a new issue:

- I keep a diary of all new issues coming up in a notebook with their launch date. Before launch I investigate them, and I keep my eye on the press for any stories about the company. But the best thing to do is find the company's website, which a Google search will usually unearth.

- I find out what the company does and its background. I then try and think: how much can the company grow after it launches on the market? What sort of strategy does it have and could it go higher?

Examples

The best way I can explain how I look at new issues, and how I decide whether to buy them or leave them alone, is by looking at two examples of new issues I bought, and two I didn't.

First, two that I bought.

Sondex

Sondex came to my attention as usual though the *IC*. I was immediately interested because it was quite an unusual company.

The first thing I did is take a look at the company's website via a Google search. I liked what I saw right away with Sondex's site, it summed up for me in a sentence on its home page what it did:

> *"Sondex is the source of downhole technology and equipment for the global oil and gas industry, supplying oilfield service companies and national oil companies worldwide."*

I liked the way they sum up their business. I can understand what they do.

Now, I don't know much about the oil industry, but it seemed fairly obvious that Sondex could grow its business as it seemed to have quite a niche market. With oil exploration on the up, it seemed Sondex products are going to be sought after.

I ended up buying Sondex a couple of weeks after it launched on the market at 130p.

It proved a wise move... six months later the shares zoomed over 200p and at the time of writing they are 230p and I'm sitting on a very nice profit!

Sondex: Following float in 2003

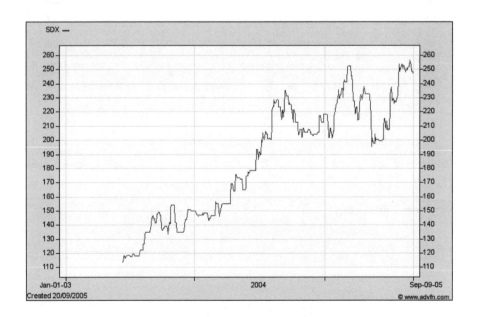

121

Dignity

I noticed this company launching on the market. It was a bit macabre I suppose as Dignity turned out to be a chain of funeral parlours. (I did wonder whether there were any share perks... such as a coffin upgrade when I eventually bite the dust!)

I did a bit of research and discovered 600,000 people a year die in the UK – that figure is quite static so it wasn't exactly a growth market. However, what I did notice was Dignity intended to grow by acquiring other funeral operations – this seemed a pretty sound strategy. I could see how earnings would grow by buying out other operators and how that would gradually lift the share price. Also, this share seemed a reasonably safe buy – after all (and sorry if this sounds awful) but people won't stop dying. I bought some for my pension fund as it looked like the type of share that would gradually keep growing in value.

I bought some at 240p and as I write the shares are 350p.

Dignity: Following float in 2004

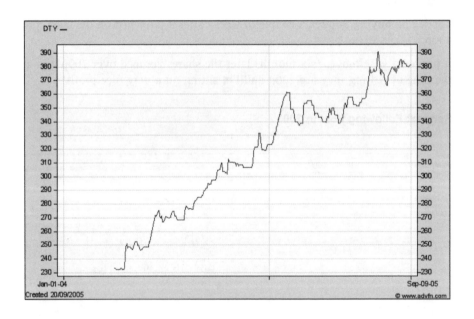

Now ones I didn't buy!

Pinewood Studios

At first glance Pinewood Studios seemed a very exciting investment. I love movies and always fancied some kind of investment in that type of business. What fun to have an investment in the movie business, and even the TV quiz show *The Weakest Link* which is filmed at Pinewood.

But then I thought to myself, films are a pretty risky business. Where is the growth coming from to really lift the share price? What if they make some flops?

There might be steady use of their studio facilities and their sets do very well, but I just couldn't see why the shares would rise that much. So I gave the shares a miss – which is just as well as, after an initial rise, they fell back. They eventually issued a dire profit warning!

Pinewood Shepperton: Following float in 2004

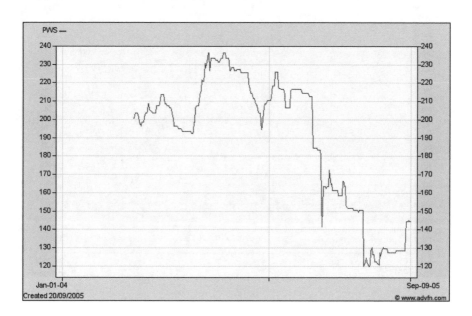

Virgin Mobile

Another one I gave a miss was Virgin Mobile. This launch on the market was, of course, high profile.

I didn't buy this one for one simple reason – intense competition in the mobile phone market. Again, I asked myself the question: where is the growth coming from short-term that will lift the share price?

The answer had to be no!

The Virgin float was also quite high publicity – and I often find the issues that come with the biggest hype are usually those to avoid. For example, the Sondex float came with very little hype at all.

Virgin Mobile: Following float in 2004

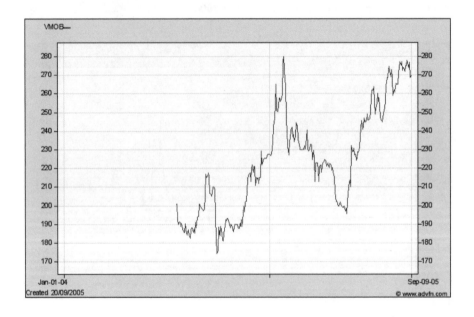

Timing

If there is a company that interests you, timing of your buy is quite crucial. I usually buy in the week after the company is floated and try and watch the price to get in at the right time. It's probably best to get in early as, if it is a good one, the price is likely to gain gradually.

If you are going for a new issue, even the good ones take time to build up a head of steam – so you may have to presume you're going to hold it for at least a year or so to get the best value.

Now a word of warning. (Have you noticed I like my warnings?)

Be careful of new issues offered to you

You may find you get letters or phone approaches from people offering you what might be called 'new issues', or 'VCI' trusts, or even offering you shares in an upcoming float.

Be careful!

The brochures all sound very appealing, and some of the shares on offer might be OK over the long-term, but some will be in dodgy one-product only companies.

Think of the new issue market like a food chain. At the bottom of the food chain are you and I. Above us are brokers, friends of brokers, fund managers, (trust fund of the fund manager's pet chihuahua), rich people, company founders, company founders' family, etc. Now, normally, shares in good new issues are like gold dust, they are snapped up by those high in the food chain. So, what does that say about new issues that have to be offered to people like us at the very bottom of the food chain? It says those issues have 'avoid' written all over them.

New issues summary

- Investigate the company on offer.
- Take a look at its website.
- Be cautious of being offered a new issue.
- Get in fairly quickly after market launch.

The joy of bids

Oh, the joy when a company you are holding gets a takeover approach.

Even better when other companies get involved and a bidding war erupts. Usually what happens is you'll wake up one morning and feel rather good, because one of your shares is up 20% as it has become a bid target. Bids usually go through at a premium of around 20% to the share price in the market, sometimes more. You'll find a news story which states the rough bid price and the share will go up to about that price.

Let's say you own shares in a company with a share price of 80p, and a bid is announced for your company at 100p.

Do you take the money and run?

Probably, unless there's reason to suspect there is going to be another bid for the company. You'll probably be able to sell at 99p and you may as well because it usually takes around three months for a bid to go through, and it's hardly worth waiting for the extra penny.

The most famous recent example was the potential takeover of **Marks & Spencer**. It looked like there was going to be a bid at the 400p level and the shares soared up to near that level. I'd have sold, but many held on. The bid fell through and the shares went down.

One of the main questions an investor asks is:

"How do I spot a bid target?"

All I can tell you is, it's extremely difficult!

There's a lot of gossip in the press about this or that company being a potential bid target. Some stories do the rounds for years. Sometimes they come true and sometimes they don't.

The real problem is if you buy a share simply because you've read somewherethat it might be a bid target, and the share has already gone up because the story is out there! What usually happens if the bid does not materialise quickly, is that the share in question will just go down again.

A bid for a company usually comes from a bigger company in the same sector that wants to snap up said company cheaply. It knocks out some competition, and enhances earnings. For example, a house builder might want to snap up another smaller house builder. Or a bank might want to swallow another bank.

Spotting a bid target is really just guesswork and you might strike lucky.

But there is no easy system to spot one. Volume perhaps is one way (which I discuss in a moment during my discussion on insider trading).

I've struck lucky maybe once every other year with a sudden increase in the value of a share I'm holding. I struck lucky recently with **Ashtenne**, a property company. Shares soared 55p after a bid from rivals Warner Estates.

My general view is don't buy a company just because you think it might be a bid target. Buy it because you like the fundamentals or technicals.

If a company you're holding ends up falling to another company at a 20% premium, just look on it as a lucky day! Just don't go chasing bid stories. A bid is more likely to come as a surprise out of the blue.

> ### Bid summary
>
> - Don't buy shares on bid rumours alone.
> - If it's in the press it might be in the price.
> - Sell the shares once the bid is agreed.
> - Don't chase bid stories.

Directors' dealings

Generally, directors are allowed to buy and sell shares in their own companies, but they are not allowed to trade in shares of their company in the six weeks preceding a results announcement (this is known as the 'closed' period). Many investors believe that by following buys or sales by directors they can make money.

But like any money making system, I don't believe it works.

I certainly think it is worth looking at directors' dealings, but I would look on a director buy as a bonus rather than a reason to buy.

The problem is that directors are usually rather enthusiastic about their companies and so might buy even if the shares are actually overvalued. Sometimes directors simply buy to try and prop up the price of their company if the share price has been falling.

For example, Robert Maxwell was busy buying shares in **Maxwell**, even though he must have known the company was in deep trouble.

They know by buying the share there will be an announcement and that could cause investors to buy in.

Look at the trade size

The key, I believe to working out whether a director buy or sell is worth following or not, is the amount of shares bought or sold in relation to that director's current holding.

For example, if a CEO of a company sells one million shares, does that mean it is time to follow suit?

Not necessarily, if, say, the director still owns fifteen million shares. He might just have needed the money to buy a better house! But if he'd sold half his stake, I would probably bail out!

It's the same with buys – always check the amount of shares a director is buying and selling against the amounts he or she holds. The bigger the proportion of shares bought compared to the amount owned is what you should look at carefully.

In early 2004 a director of Big Yellow bought 500,000 shares in the company, significantly increasing his stake.

Big Yellow: September 2000 – September 2005

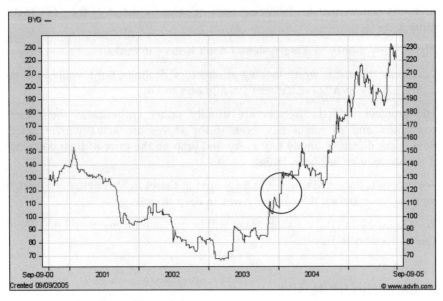

I would be tempted to buy here. That's because he is significantly increasing the amount of shares he owns in the company.

In fact I did buy on this occasion at 110p – and the buy proved a winner as the shares soon ran up to 200p.

It can sometimes be a good sign if a director buys, say, £20,000 worth of shares if they only already hold a small amount. Not all directors are wealthy, and £20,000 might be quite a big investment for a director of a smaller company.

Here's one example of when following a director could have led you to lose everything!

Henlys Group: September 2000 – September 2005

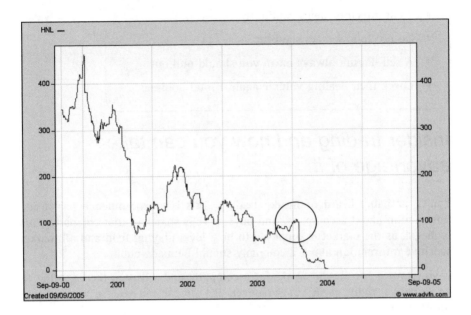

A director of **Henlys Group**, Mr Gillespie, bought 10,000 shares in the company at 101p on January 13th 2004. I'm sure many directors' dealings followers would have bought in after his buy. The shares had gone from 60p to 101p, and everything looked rosy.

Amazingly, just two weeks later there was a profit warning and the shares went into freefall, tumbling in a few days to 30p. Much worse was to come and by June (just five months after he'd bought) the shares were worth... er nothing!

Monitoring directors' dealings

It is easy to discover when directors have bought or sold. ADVFN has a 'directors' dealings' list which updates whenever a director's trade is announced.

If you are going to follow directors' dealing, it is better to monitor them on ADVFN rather than wait for the dealings to be announced, say in a Sunday newspaper or a magazine.

Note	I don't think there are any firm conclusions to be drawn from directors' deals. Look on them a bit suspiciously and don't follow them slavishly.

> ### Director's dealings' summary
>
> - Treat directors' deals cautiously.
> - Do not follow them slavishly.
> - A sell doesn't always mean you should pull out.
> - Check their dealing volume against total holdings.

Insider trading and how you can take advantage of it

You've probably heard of insider trading. This is when someone has inside information about a company, and buys or sells shares in that company. This is illegal, as the market is supposed to be a level playing field and all market sensitive information about a company should be made public.

If you have a friend who works for a company and tells you there's going to be a bid, a rights issue, or whatever, it's illegal for you to act on that information.

In practice, when it comes to bids or similar price shifting announcements, loads of people end up finding out about it well before anything is announced. Of course it is human nature to gossip so quite soon hundreds of people know about it. And, given human nature again, as you can imagine many can't resist the temptation to buy, illegally or not.

My personal, and probably controversial, view is that I don't think insider trading should be illegal. My argument goes something like this:

1. Insider trading is currently illegal to protect the small investor, who doesn't get to hear the inside information. He misses out. But while sensitive information is known by some people, but not acted upon, that creates a false market in the shares – whose price is *not* reflecting all the information known about the company. This is not how efficient markets are supposed to behave. At some point the information *will* become public knowledge, at which point the small investor will *always* lose out to the market professionals who can trade much faster. Except, the small investor could end up losing out more as the sudden adjustment in share price could be far greater than if the share price had been allowed to adjust slowly and steadily as the (inside) information percolated throughout the market.

2. The definition of 'inside information' is not as clear-cut as it may seem. An analyst may visit a finance director at a company: they have lunch, things are said, things are not said (often, what is not said is as informative as what is!). Later, the analyst chats with a fund manager and recommends the latter

buy shares in the company. When asked why, the analyst just taps his nose. Well, honestly, it's absurd trying to regulate activity like this? Is the analyst to be arrested under the Brussels No Nose Tapping Directive #1664?

3. Insider trading is notoriously difficult to prove. So what is the point of having a law that is almost impossible to enforce and therefore never used (even though insider trading is rife)?

4. It gets worse. It's difficult enough to prove insider trading in the stock market as it is, but no self-respecting insider trader today is going to ring up a stock broker and say, "Quick, get me 100k shares in Dodgy Widgets". Instead they're going to hotfoot it to the CFD or spread betting markets – which are very difficult to monitor.

5. I don't care if someone makes a few quid on inside knowledge. It doesn't bother me.

OK, rant over!

Companies are usually forced to put out announcements if their share prices suddenly rocket for no reason, either to state they know nothing about the rise or state there is something happening.

Listen up – Naked Trader Inside Tip

The thing is, you *can* benefit from insider trading perfectly legally. I did it myself recently.

How?

You must watch volumes – that is the number of shares traded. If a share's trading volume is way above the usual number of shares traded in the company, and the price is starting to rise, you can bet your chickens something's up.

The best way to catch abnormal volumes is to watch volumes in shares you know – and watch all the time. If a share you know usually trades 100,000 a day and then suddenly starts trading in millions, that's a signal for you to exclaim, "By jove!", to grab your deerstalker hat, pipe and magnifying glass and start investigating.

You should be looking for many trades coming in (rather than one big trade which could be an institutional buy), a sign of lots of people buying in ahead of something.

For example, I bought **Highbury House** at 6.75p because it was in my watchlist and I suddenly saw trades coming through for 500,000 shares, instead of the usual 50,000 or 100,000. I then saw the market makers raising their price and began to see the trade volume lift to ten or twelve times normal amounts. I figured those buying in wouldn't be spending quite so much if they didn't think something was about to happen.

So I bought in quickly and then saw even more trades pile in as the share rose. The share started to rise so fast that a few days later the company had to put out a statement that it was in talks that could lead to an offer being made.

I gratefully sold at that point for 9p, taking a nice, quick 20% profit. So I profited from insider trading... without ever being an insider trader!

Note The moral of the story is: watch for those unusual trades and the bigger volumes. But do check the bulletin boards just in case the volumes are caused by a tip or a news story.

This only works if the volumes are coming in on no obvious news!

However if a share you follow is suddenly dealing in much bigger volume than normal, it may well be worth buying in. Nothing like a bit of perfectly legal insider trading.

So maybe now you see why I'm not against it. If there was absolutely no insider trading ever, volumes would stay as normal and the share would only rise on the day of the announcement, but move much too quickly for non-day traders to take advantage of.

Building a portfolio

How do you go about building a decent portfolio? The secret is diversity, i.e. make sure the shares you invest in are in different sectors of the market.

For example, if most of your shares were in telecoms companies, and the whole telecoms market got hit by poor market sentiment, your portfolio could suddenly tumble.

But if you have a good mix of sectors, and different varieties of shares, there is less chance of sudden big losses.

The £7,000 (ISA) starter portfolio

Here's a few ideas of the kind of shares to go for in a starting line up of shares for a brand new portfolio. I've gone for a £7,000 starting figure as:

1. this is the maximum amount you can put in a self-select ISA; and

2. this is about the right amount of money for a new investor to put in who has the money to spare.

If you are married you could put in £14,000, as you can have two ISAs between you.

Those putting in much less than this are going to be hard pushed to create a balanced portfolio. After dealing costs, it really isn't worth buying much less than £1,000 worth of shares. With around £7,000 you can create a lower risk fund because you can diversify much more easily.

Naked Trader Starter Balanced Portfolio

FTSE 100: £1,000

Mid cap: £2,000

High yield: £1,000

Small cap: £1,000

Chart breaker/momentum: £1,000

Risky gamble: £1,000

This is the kind of balanced portfolio with a bit of risk thrown in that I'd recommend to a new investor.

And you don't have to buy all the shares at once – in fact don't! Try and find two or three shares in each category and watch closely until you feel the time is right to buy.

Note

If you're just beginning trading, don't be tempted to put more into the risky gamble shares!

Strategies

Recovery plays

Some of my biggest gains have come from finding recovery plays.

These are companies that have been struggling, but are turning their businesses around. If you can get in early enough in the turnaround, there are potentially huge profits.

But isn't backing a recovery play the same as catching a falling knife?

No, there are differences. Catching the knife just means buying a share when it's still going down. A recovery play is completely different. I am looking for definite signs of a recovery before buying in – rather than buying in just because the share has suddenly fallen.

How do I find those?

It would normally be a company where:

- The **shares have dropped** over a long while (maybe a year or so) by, say, 40-70%.

- I would first be alerted by the company's **share price stabilizing** and then maybe starting to rise a bit.

- I then like to see the company putting out statements that show it is **addressing the problems** that caused the drop in its share price in the first place.

- I also like to see **changes of personnel,** and maybe a new, more experienced management team coming on board.

- And I definitely like to see a slow and **steady recovery in the share price** before buying in, preferably coupled with signs of institutions buying in and directors too.

- If that's also followed by a **company statement giving out confidence**, then it could be a good thing!

Mothercare

A good example is Mothercare – the retailer that sells baby gear. It had a torrid time between 2001 and early 2003, when it was in 'catching knife' territory. It came out with profit warning after profit warning, and whinged on about warehouse problems. Shares slumped from more than 300p all the way down to 85p. I'd kept an eye on it without buying over those years.

It came onto my radar as a possible recovery play in late January 2003, when the head cheese bought shares. That didn't convince me totally, but then in March the company really started taking action, sacking its finance director and installing a new one. The finance director of any company is an important position, and I realised the company was taking some tough action to turn the business around. In late March, the new finance director bought shares and the head cheese bought more.

Now it was really on my radar – the new FD obviously liked what he saw in the accounts he was looking at.

Then in May the company reported a big loss – but with it came a statement which I liked the look of. The CEO announced he had tackled distribution problems, improved sales costs, and was focusing on making sure its in-town outlets, that had been neglected, boomed again. He also closed fifteen underperforming outlets and said trading was strong.

The shares started to rise and I bought in. The share was giving out all the right signs of an excellent recovery play. I bought at 130p. I could have bought at 85p just a few weeks previously, but at that point I simply wasn't sure about it. And that was fine – better to let the next man grab a few points and wait till all the signs are there, than buying in too hastily.

The shares quickly ran all the way back up to the 300p area, at which point I banked the rather nice profits.

Mothercare: September 2000 – September 2005

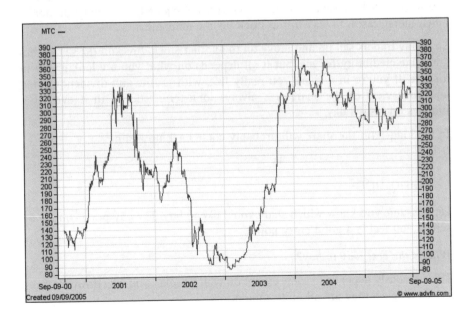

Better to travel than to arrive

A well known saying is: "Better to travel than to arrive." In the stock market, this can mean it is often better to buy a share a few weeks before results are announced and sell on the day of the announcement – even if the results are good.

Quite often shares that have risen a fair bit before results, tumble on the days afterwards. It's because the good results were anticipated, so there might not be much more reason to stay in the stock for the moment.

So, many traders sell up and move on to another stock. I reckon the saying has got some credibility for me, but it all depends on what you are looking for in a share. If you're in a share you really like, with profits and dividends rising and your view of the share was always long-term, stick with it even if it tumbles on results day.

In the long-term the share will probably come back up again.

Dealing tips

Let's assume you know which share you'd like to buy. The buy price you see on screen you feel is a good entry point.

What's the best way to buy?

This obviously depends to some extent on which broker you use. However, from my experience they are all quite similar.

Careful with the share code

After you press the 'trade' or 'enter order' button to make a trade, the first thing is (obviously) to enter the share code of the company you want to trade. Do this carefully!

One friend of mine wanted to buy Retail Decisions – the code was RTD. He was trying to buy the shares quickly and by mistake typed in TRD. He ended up buying Triad Group. There is nothing you can do to reverse a mistake like that. A big mistake as it happened, because RTD went on to triple in value while TRD did nothing at all. Ouch!

Order type

The dealing page should give you a few options of how you want the order to be executed. For example, 'at best' (also called 'at market'), 'limit', 'quote and deal', 'stop'.

The main thing to remember is: don't deal 'at best' (or 'at market'). Always use the limit facility, especially if the share is moving fast. If you don't, the share could whizz-up before your broker has dealt and you will end up paying a high price. Before you deal, think how much more you are prepared to pay for the share than is shown on the screen.

Company size matters

Buying a FTSE share is very different from buying a smaller share – let's start with buying larger shares.

Check the spread

Firstly please make sure it's at least after 8.30am and the spread is tight (i.e. the gap between the bid and offer prices is not too wide). Often until 9am the spreads can be ridiculous, and you could be caught out. For example, say you wanted to buy shares in BSkyB. The previous night the shares could have closed at 690-691. At 8am they could be 650-750! If you put an order in you could end up paying 750p instead of 691p, an expensive mistake.

Place a limit

Anyhow, let's say it's after 9am and the BSkyB offer price is 691p. This is easy dealing: it's a FTSE 100 company and you can buy as many shares as you want. The price might tick up one or two pence while you're dealing, so put in an order with a limit of about 694p, just in case.

In the old days, by telephone, you would have instructed your broker to: 'Buy *x* shares in BSkyB, limit 694.' Online, depending on the design of your broker's order page, you would click the 'limit' button, and type '694' into the limit box. This instructs the broker to buy *x* shares in BSkyB at the lowest price possible, but not to pay more than 694p.

Let's take another example. You decide you want to buy Hydro. You look at ADVFN and you obtain the following info:

- The selling price is 116p, the buying price 120p.

- You want to buy 3,000 shares, but the normal market size is 500 shares. It means you want more shares than the MMs have to deal in, so you may have to pay more than 120p. Possibly 121p.

In this case, you may want to put in a limit order of 121p if you really want the shares. If you put in a limit order of 120p, the MMs could reject most of your order and then put the price up!

Each market maker sets an 'electronic dealing size' on every stock. This means sometimes when you press the 'buy' button your trade will go through instantaneously. Depending on your broker's service, when you press 'buy', a window pop up telling you the buying price and giving you fifteen seconds to accept or decline.

Say you're buying a smaller company; you may just get a notice saying:'"Trade pending'. What happens now is your broker will have to get on the phone to a market maker to deal the shares for you. He will call the market maker that is in favour at the time and try and get you a good price. This usually takes about five minutes. You'll then see your trade come up on the real-time prices feed. You can press 'order status' to confirm the price you got.

If you set a limit on your deal, your broker may not be able to get you that price and might phone you.

For example, recently I wanted 2,000 shares in a company and the price was 250p to buy. I set a limit of 251p, but a minute after I put the order in, the price went to 253p. Rats.

My broker phoned. "I can get you 254p if you want to deal now, " he said. I agreed as I really wanted the shares.

Note You can see here it was important I'd put on a limit. If I hadn't, I could have ended up paying more for the shares and certainly I would have had little control over the price I eventually got.

Here's another good tip:

Naked Trader Dummy Orders

When buying a share over the net the chances are it'll get dealt electronically. What normally happens is a little window opens up telling you the price you've been offered for your buy or sell and there is usually a fifteen second countdown clock.

Note: you do not have to accept this offer.

What I'm getting at is you can do a 'dummy' buy or sell. This is what I do to check to see whether it's the right time to buy a share. This works especially well on Squaregain's share dealing system, but could work well elsewhere too.

Here's what to do:

Put in a buy order of, say, 100 shares. Let's say the share's offer quote is 200p. You are offered 198p. I would worry a bit as the market maker is happy to give me a *much* better price. 199.9p is okay but 198p is a bit suspicious!

I then look at part of the window which says 'maximum trade size'.

- If this said **500 shares** I would be interested. It would mean the market maker is only offering a small amount of shares so the share is in demand.

- If the maximum dealing size was **100,000 shares,** the market maker is obviously desperate to get rid of shares and I would not buy!

Recommended reading

Stephen Eckett on Online Investing is really a must read, especially for the new investor. Some not-to-be-missed dealing tips, along with answers to pretty much any question regarding online trading. I can safely say this is a must buy!

Picking undervalued shares – my secret!

All the best things in life are simple, and I think the system I use to pick out undervalued shares is simplicity itself.

Here's what I do.

You are a billionaire

I use this system after researching any company that looks of interest. I pretend that I am a multi-billionaire investor and could buy any company or as many companies as I want to. But of course I want to buy them on the cheap. I want to buy companies that are making profits, but if I pay cash for the companies I know these profits would probably grow. Over a few years I'd get back what I paid for the company and start to make a lot of money on top.

The idea behind my system is: if I decide it's worth splashing out a small part of my billions to buy the company then I've decided the company is cheap. And if that's the case, I should buy the shares because, if I'm right, sooner or later someone will buy the company or the share price will go up anyway.

So how can I work out whether to splash out a small part of my billions on snapping up a company?

The first thing to look at is the profit the company makes; and the second is the market capitalisation. In my billionaire role, my rule of thumb for how much the company might cost me to buy is the market capitalisation. So if a company's market cap is £50 million, that's how much the market currently thinks the company is worth.

ADVFN provides the market cap and the profit on its 'Quote' page on the same line, so they are easy to find.

Screenshot from ADVFN Quotes page

Fenner(FENR)								Click for Fundamentals	
Name	Symbol	Market			Type		ISIN	Description	
Fenner	LSE:FENR	London Stock Exchange			Equity		GB0003345054	ORD 25P	

Change	Change %	Cur	Bid	Offer	High	Low	Open	Volume	Chg Time	
↓ -0.25	-0.2%	154.25	154.0	154.5	156.25	154.25	156.0	33,582	14:59	XD

Sector	Turnover (m)	Profit (m)	EPS - Basic	PE ratio	Mkt Cap (m)	NMS
Engineering & Machinery	260.595	6.395	2.23	-	242.6	10000

Type	Size	Price	Tr.Time	Units
O	1,000	154.2	14:19	GBX

As a billionaire I don't really care about complicated financial ratios and all that twaddle. What I want to know is: how much do you want for your company, and what are the profits?

Putting it simply: if a company is making profits of £10 million and its market cap is £100 million, that would interest me.

But if a company makes a £10 million profit and is capitalised at £200 million, then I'm not so interested – even if it has some kind of stupendous product that is about to dramatically raise profits. I don't want to spend £200 million to get profits of £10 million whatever the prospects.

The best thing I can do here is give an example of a company that I bought and made great profits on – one that I bought using my billionaire's hat.

Carr's Milling

The company was Carr's Milling.

Why would I buy it as a billionaire?

Well, the market cap was roughly £35 million (this gives a guide as to what I might have to pay). Yet it was making profits of more than £5 million already, and profits were on the way up. The company makes flour, so has a good steady market too.

That looked pretty good to me, especially as the company was obviously growing. Profits could easily become £7-£8 million or more in a couple of years, especially as the company was buying others at a good price. Imagine £8 million profits. Now we're talking really cheap.

Being an imaginary billionaire really helped! I bought at 380p, and the shares have stormed higher to the late 500s as I write.

Carr's Milling: September 2000 – September 2005

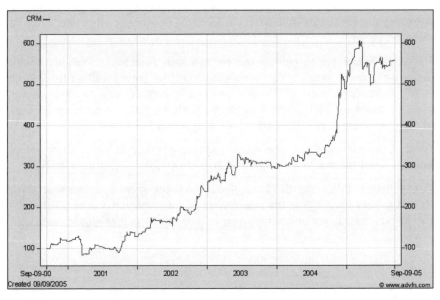

Be wary of loss-making companies

I am sometimes, like everyone, tempted by companies that are making losses. I often look at them and see a company that makes a loss, but has a market cap of £71 million because it has some kind of product that investors think will take off.

But would I buy it?

It's possible the product will work out, but I have no interest in paying over the odds for the possible future potential. I'd much rather buy a company whose profits are already booming. I guess that's why I hardly ever buy a loss-maker.

Note So next time you buy a share, have a good think. Would you buy the company yourself if you had the money? Not sure? Well, if you're not, don't buy the shares!

Look at the big picture

And I'm not talking *Lord of the Rings* here!

I believe you have to look at the whole picture of a share before diving into a buy. This is particularly relevant if you rely on chart signals to buy a stock, especially if it's a smaller company. I don't personally believe in just looking at chart signals, breakouts or whatever. So here's a story to illustrate what I'm going on about.

A chartist friend called me up and he was rather excited. "I've just bought Highbury House!" he said. "I've been watching it for weeks waiting for it to get to 12p and today's the day." He then went on to explain why his chart showed it was a cracking buy. Something to do with a double bottom or a magic triangle, or some such. "I'll have a look at it," I said.

Years of experience often help when deciding whether to buy a share or not. And it's often the smallest things that give out ominous warning signals.

I immediately didn't like the look of one fact; the spread on the shares was 10.5-11.5. Yet those buying the shares were being given 11p. Curious, I thought. The market makers seemed very happy to part with stock at good prices.

What's worse was there was an awful lot of big selling going on. When you see someone selling 140,000 shares the day before results, you do wonder.

Then I found out, by looking at the last statement from the company, that its results had been delayed – and that's often a sign all is not well. In fact, I discovered the results were due out the next day!

It was now 4pm. With the markets due to shut in half an hour I reckoned things did not look good for my friend's buy. I called him back. "I'd get out," I said. "Heavy selling, generous buying prices, it just doesn't feel right."

He decided to hold on. Fair enough!

The next day dawned and the company announced a fall in profits. Shares slumped to 8.5p.

A day later and my friend called me. "I took my losses," he said. "Oh no!" I said. "I've just bought some!" There was no way he should have taken his losses there and then. You've always got to let the market settle before selling in a panic.

Again, he wasn't looking at the big picture – a new picture – being painted. I'd bought some at just over 9p because I'd just seen an announcement that the directors had all waded into the market buying shares. It was certainly a short-term vote of confidence in the company. All those buys would be in the press the next day and probably prompt further buys. Also the company now looked undervalued even given the profit warning. And there was no way Highbury was likely to go bust short-term.

Over the next few days the shares rose back up to 11p. Then 12p! The 12p price was good enough for me and I sold, grabbing quick profits of £2,400. I did right to sell because a few weeks later the shares began to slump again.

So I reiterate – look at the whole picture before you buy or sell a share. Are you selling or buying in a panic or are you unemotionally looking at the facts before you?

Have you checked everything – such as market maker prices, news stories, etc? All the small things add up to the big picture.

My Real Trades And Strategies

My trades and how I picked them

I've already pointed out some of my winning trades and how I picked them, but I thought at this point it might be handy to look at some more of my trades, and why and how I picked them.

I obviously picked them all because I thought they were going up. (A Naked Trader Insightful Statement Of The Obvious!) But, as with all trades I make, a lot of thought went in before buying.

I hope some of my thought processes might help you see why I picked them, and how you could use the same kind of thoughts when you're looking for shares to buy. I cover how I discovered the company in the first place, what I did to research it and why I finally made a decision to buy.

Burren Energy

Burren Energy: September 2002 – September 2005

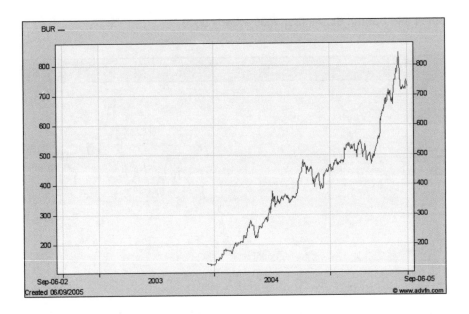

I first came across this oil exploration company when it was floated on the market at the end of 2003. As mentioned, when I see new issues coming onto the market (I check the *Investors Chronicle* for them) I usually put them on a separate monitor and keep an eye on their progress.

Oil exploration companies are, of course, risky. A good oil find and they can storm up; a bad drilling report and they can plummet. So this was firmly in the risky category.

I didn't buy for quite a while, but simply watched the shares gradually move upwards.

I noticed the drilling reports getting more and more interesting, and share trading volumes were also picking up. I liked the fact they were discovering quite a lot of oil in the same region – this is often the precursor to finding more.

With the oil price rising strongly, and their area of the world producing good quantities of oil, this looked like a good one.

I decided it was time to take a chance and bought for 239p in April 2004. The share never looked back. It joined the FTSE 250 by September, and in just a few months I ended up doubling my money as Burren soared to 480p. As I write you can make that nearly treble as the shares have soared over 800p.

Gibbs and Dandy

Gibbs and Dandy: September 2000 – Early 2005

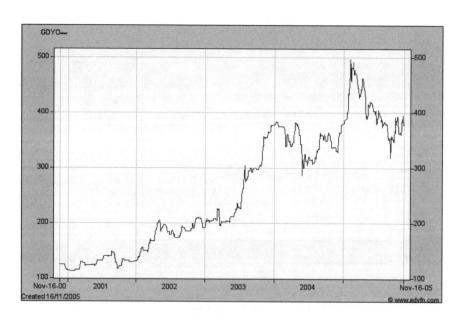

This one came to my attention on January 6th, 2005.

I happened to be trawling through a list of directors' dealings on ADVFN, when I spotted the finance director of this company had snapped up £15,000 worth of shares to add to his already very large holding. The thing that interested me was that he already held around £2 million worth of shares, but rather than taking profits on quite a sizeable profit he was happy to add more.

So I had a good look at the company. On doing my research, I discovered the company was what some might regard as a slightly boring one – a chain of builders' merchants. But with many people not moving because property prices were stagnating, and doing up their houses instead, this looked interesting.

Even more interesting to see was that Gibbs was buying up other similar merchants and slowly expanding their chain. With profits and dividends rising fast, and some very bullish statements coming from the company, this looked a winner.

On top of all that, the share price chart looked very strong and it was busting out through previous highs.

So I waded in and bought quite a few at 413p. A few weeks later the shares touched 500p.

VP Group

VP Group: September 2000 – September 2005

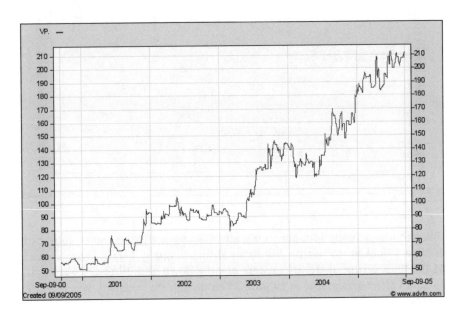

This one attracted my attention in June 2004. I found it while scanning company results one quiet morning, and I liked what I saw.

Like Gibbs, VP was slowly and carefully expanding its equipment rental business. I like slowly – it means they weren't building up debt too quickly.

Profits were up to £8.9 million from £7.5 million – a healthy increase. The dividend was hiked up – also a good sign. But best of all, despite such decent profits the company was only capitalised at £75 million. I would expect the company to be worth at least £90 million on such profits.

Given profits could easily rise further, this looked a no-brainer. I bought in at 129p, just before a director also snapped up some.

Shares slowly but surely rose, and by early 2005 they got to 200p.

Dart Group

Dart Group: September 2000 – September 2005

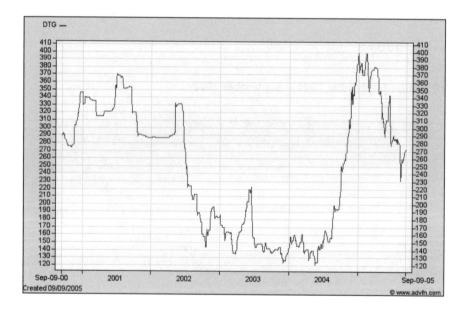

This one was actually brought to my attention by a website reader quite early in 2004. It looked interesting, but as an airline company I wasn't sure about it. At the time, airline share prices were coming down and oil prices were going up, and I erred on the side of caution, even though the company was reporting impressive results.

I could have bought at 150p, but I put it on my watchlist and saw it gradually climb. Higher and higher. In fact it nearly doubled before I bought at 296p!

I cursed when I finally bought, but it all looked good, even with the doubling of the share price.

Profits had risen to an impressive £11 million from £7.4 million, and with a great rise in the dividend it looked attractive. Reading the reports, the management looked impressive. I discovered Dart ran passenger plane services from the north of the UK; but the planes could double up in just a few minutes into freight carriers. Now I really liked the sound of that – basically a plane that could be used nearly 24 hours a day.

I suppose some would say it's risky buying a share that's just doubled in value, but the buy worked out and it rose to 400p by early 2005. With a good profit to take I did bank them. Just as well because in mid 2005, the company decided to switch to an AIM listing meaning ISA investors like me were forced to sell.

Sondex

See chart 'Sondex: Following float in 2003' on page 121

This one I found from a list of those companies floating on the main market. I watched it debut at about 120p in December 2003, and shortly thereafter bought in at 130p.

It wasn't my sort of company, really, as it was losing money, but rules are made to be broken!

It seemed to have a good niche market supplying oil companies with equipment. As I was reading a lot about the oil and exploration boom, this company seemed to fit in well with the rest of my portfolio at the time.

It went up quickly to 200p, where I considered taking profits. However, after reading an interview with the boss of the company in a newspaper I stayed in as he seemed very bullish. The price rose to 230p by early 2005.

RPC

RPC: September 2000 – September 2005

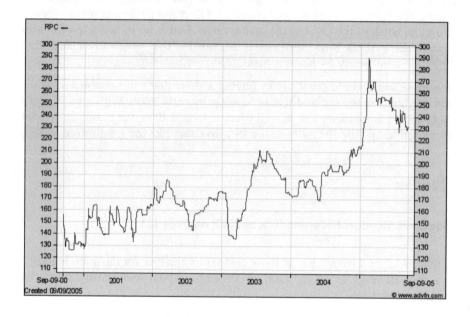

I bought this one at 203p in November 2004. I found it on a 52 week Breakout list on ADVFN's premium lists.

At first glance it seemed a fairly boring packaging company, but on an in-depth look I liked it a lot. There was good buying volume coming in. The market cap of £245 million against profits of £25 million looked too low. And the other thing I wondered was: could it be a bid target for another packaging company?

It was also ready to grow itself and had just bought a huge European packaging company. That purchase alone made me feel RPC was a company about to go places.

By early 2005 shares had raced up to near the 300p mark, and I eventually sold in mid 2005 at 272p.

Vanco

See chart 'Vanco: September 2000 – September 2005' on page 83

I discovered this IT company from a small article in one of the Sunday papers. I didn't immediately buy, but put it on my watchlist.

I researched it and liked the look of the business model. I discovered it ran IT networks for a variety of top name companies and it was winning new contracts.

This looked a company on the up – but its shares had stalled for quite a while at 181p. I decided to watch and wait for any sign of upward momentum. I can be quite patient and that often brings rewards.

In October 2003, it suddenly started to move higher, so I bought at 185p. My wait paid off as the company's share price started to rocket as other investors took notice of its business model. I sold at 280p. I bought back quite quickly again and by mid 2005 the shares were over 400p.

I hope all these examples will help you when you are looking at your own shares to buy.

In all cases I'd always have a look at the chart, news stories, profits, turnover, earnings per share and everything else I can find as reported elsewhere in the book.

Note

Even when I like a share it doesn't mean I buy it right away. Patience is a virtue when it comes to share buying.

My favourite share ever!

My best profit-making share of all time has to be the housebuilder, Costain. I've made more than £40,000 in profits from this share alone over the last five years.

I first bought Costain in December 2001 at 12p, as a possible and risky recovery play. It quickly doubled in value and I sold at 24p.

Someone on the ADVFN bulletin board posted my comment on Costain. I wrote on my website:

> *"Costain is my pick of a share for 2002 that could easily double."*

I'm glad I did!

- I bought back at 22p and sold again at 34p.
- Bought again at 28p and sold at 38p.
- Bought again at 32p and sold at 44p.
- And as I write I have bought yet again at 46p and hoping for a new rise to 58p.

Costain: September 2000 – September 2005

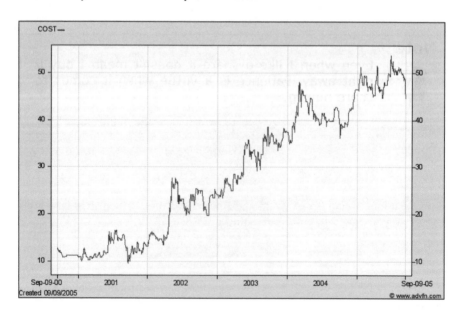

What is it about the share that I liked and why did I keep coming back?

Quite simply, it's always looked great value. I keep looking at it, and with my billionaire's hat on, I know I would buy the company in a flash. Even more simply, as Costain grew, it just kept winning more (and quite large) contracts for building work from (deep pocketed) utility companies.

Even better, the share moved in a recognisable pattern. Usually rising 7-10 points before investors (like me) were tempted to take profits. This easy to read pattern meant it was simple to take profits and buyback at the right time.

I was also safe in the knowledge that a profit warning was unlikely... and this brings me to another trading secret, and that is:

Sleep-at-night shares

Every portfolio needs sleep-at-night shares.

What I mean by this is a number of rock solid, profit-making shares that are unlikely to go down very much. They won't set the world alight either, but are more likely to go up slowly but surely, steadily creating wealth. I think three sleep-at-night companies should form the bedrock of any portfolio.

The best examples are to be found in the construction sector, and companies who make money from renting out properties.

Construction companies are great as the contracts they win last a long time and this generally means they keep getting paid out over the long-term and so are 'sleep at night'.

Costain is one good example. Another favourite of mine is Kier Group, which, like Costain, gradually rises in value as it, too, picks up its fair share of contracts. And again it goes up and down in regular patterns. As I write I'm in at 840p expecting to take profits at 920p.

In a different sector, a good company is Dignity as mentioned earlier. It's a funeral parlour chain – I'm afraid people always die, which means the company will always have a steady income. It is unlikely to be hit by a profit warning unless someone invents a cure for death! It can also expand its profits by buying up other smaller funeral parlours.

So have a look around the market and find at least one or two sleep-at-nights. I promise you, you will end up sleeping a lot better!

The Nervous Nineties

I've found over the years it's worth looking at shares that are about to hit, or are already in, the 'Nervous Nineties'. By that I mean a stock that's somewhere around 87-96p or 187-196p etc.

That's because a round number like 100 or 200 seems to create a big barrier for investors. Shares that are climbing often reach close to the barrier but can't get through it.

The reason for looking at buying shares in the Nervous Nineties is that if the barrier is breached – and the share goes through 100 or 200, etc – they often climb fast because the barrier has been removed. It's often worth topping up after the barrier has been breached to catch the next wave up.

Of course, I'm not saying buy every share before and after a whole number barrier. The right fundamentals and rising chart pattern should be in place. It should be a share you want to buy.

And if you're sure about it, it's worth being patient, as shares often get close to the whole number, then come back, try again then come back a few times.

Fenner

For example, I bought a company called Fenner at 87p or so, as it was breaking out of a previous range. It went up to 97p, then dipped back below 90p. Then it had another go and failed. But on the next go it pushed up above 100p.

It stayed there for a while and then headed up to 107p at which point I bought some more shares. It then tested 100p again but I held on as 100p had become a major support level. This proved the case and ever since then it's been up, up and away...

Fenner: September 2000 – September 2005

Hunting

Another example is Hunting, which I bought at 185p. It has behaved in a similar way. It went up to 195p, looked like it was going to break through the 200p barrier, only to drop off back to 185p. I suspect another attempt will be made which could be unsuccessful; but a third attempt could bring it over 200p. If that happens, then it's likely to whiz up to 220p.

Newsflash: Hunting now heading for 300p!

Of course, it can be risky playing the Nervous Nineties – the share could have broken out prematurely and could retreat. So sometimes, if I'm not sure, I wait for the round number barrier to be broken.

Hunting: September 2000 – September 2005

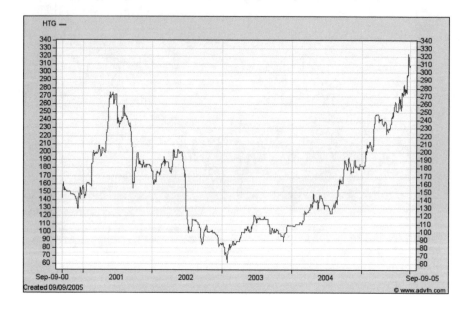

White Young Green

This happened with White Young Green. I bought at 205p, after the Nervous Nineties barrier had been broken. The share went to 220p then re-tested 200p again. After that, there was no stopping the party and the shares whizzed up to 270p, at which point I happily sold.

It's all to do with human psychology. These round numbers nearly always stop shares in their tracks. But onc e that round number is broken, optimism abounds.

The same I think is true of shares in a downtrend. A break below the round number can see quick falls as it erodes confidence further.

Note I'm always aware of the round number area. It pays to watch shares closely that are around this level, and if you get it right there can be big rewards.

Ooh, you tease

There are certain shares that can only be described as teasers. They're a bit like some girls I used to know. They give you a bit of a come on, but then don't deliver the goods. I'm sure you know what I mean.

There they are, all lovely looking with their shiny profits and enticing dividends. Some even come with low, plunging...err, PEs. Add the come hither share price behaviour: going up nicely, and just about to soar higher. And you're all ready to pounce (and buy).

Then suddenly, just when you think you're building up a nice relationship, it all goes cold.

But the shares will carry on teasing you, every now and again going up a few points. Hope swells back and things look great again. But then they disappoint time and time again, and the share price sinks back.

It's happened to me a few times, I've been teased endlessly, But I've learned my lesson now and it's not going to happen again.

Hill & Smith

The biggest tease of all time for me is a company called Hill & Smith. It always promised me we had a future together, but it was all just sweet talk.

It showed me lovely profits and a small market cap. It had a seductive low PE ratio, a nice little dividend and a promise of more profits to come.

So I bought in a couple of years ago at 100p. It even went to 110p during the honeymoon, but then it fell back. And time and again it rose a few pence, only to come back every time. We had a falling out and I sold.

But I couldn't resist its allure (I'll have you know this is painful to relate), and bought back in again twice more. Both times my hopes were dashed, as every time it promised a lovely rise it fell back refusing to go above 112p.

I should have just taken it off my monitor! But I can't help but keeping an eye on it.

I nearly bought again. It actually went above 110p and I was soooo tempted. Then it went to 120p and I thought I had missed out. But, oh no, not Hill & Smith! It clicked back to below 120p.

My long-term relationship has left me with nothing but burnt hopes and small losses.

Hill & Smith: September 2000 – September 2005

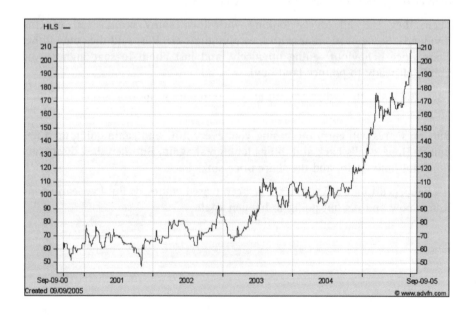

The lessons

What can we learn from these types of shares?

We just have to realise that some shares are going to remain unloved by the market and private investors, and will continue to trade at undervalued prices. There's nothing we can do about it except move on.

So how on earth do you avoid a teaser?

Well, it's not easy. You'll know quite quickly though – you'll begin to get irritated and want to end it but you can't.

But you've just got to get out and move on. You have to recognise that you're being teased. The solution: sell, and then cut all ties to ensure it all doesn't happen again.

The only time to get back into a teaser is if it really breaks out of its small range. Let it rise up quite a few points before buying in. Let it prove itself and show that the market is taking real interest. That's when it stops becoming a teaser and becomes a winner. Suddenly everyone wants to know and it'll soar at last.

For example, **Havelock Europa** used to be a teaser for me. I kept buying in the low 90s but it refused to budge much. So I gave up and waited. It suddenly burst through 100p and I bought at 105p or thereabouts, and it's now at 130p.

So I guess what I'm saying is, if a share is sitting there doing nothing, get out and use your money elsewhere and be patient. Get back in when the teasing is over. Don't worry about missing out on a few points.

Postscript: My biggest tease of all time, Hill & Smith, finally broke out at the beginning of 2005. It broke above 120p, and raced up, almost without pause, to 176p. As I say above, when a teaser finally gives up teasing and breaks out of its range, it can soar.

10

Learning From Mistakes

My biggest disaster of all time

Learning from mistakes is always useful. Learning from other people's mistakes is both useful and painless. And, admit it, we all like a bit of *schadenfreude*: "oh, you didn't do that, you didn't, you couldn't have done, you total plonker!" Okay, this mistake still lives with me every day. Perhaps its re-telling will help to exorcise the demons.

Whatever, as the Americans would say: I'd like to share this with you...

My purchase of Coffee Republic Shares in 2001, and my subsequent inability to stem losses arising from that purchase, is the best example I can give of the many classic mistakes it is possible to make as an investor.

Coffee Republic: September 2000 – September 2005

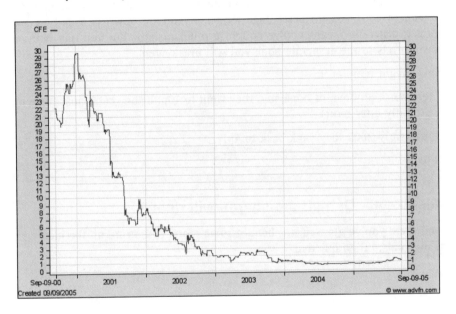

Mistake 1 – Did not do proper research

I bought the shares at 27p in late 2000. I hardly did any research and bought on a whim.

I always enjoyed coffee and liked coffee bars, and even wanted to set one up myself. The shares were having a good run, but I ignored the fact that the company was making big losses, and they'd have to sell an awful lot of coffee to ever make a profit.

By early 2001, the shares had dropped to 20p. No problem, I'd wisely set a stop loss of 22p.

Mistake 2 – Ignored my stop loss

Err, except I didn't sell. (Prat!)

Instead of selling up, I crossed my fingers – which actually worked for a time and the shares went up to 22p again.

But by late 2001, they had sunk all the way down to 8p.

Mistake 3 – 'Averaged down'

At this point, not only did I hold onto the shares as they went further and further down, but I compounded my error by the classic mistake: averaging down.

The idea of averaging down is to buy more shares at a lower price, which brings down the average cost of your total holding in the company. It's like magic – it reduces your loss (in percentage terms). Averaging down is usually a bad idea. It generally means you've bought a rubbish share, but you buy more at lower levels in the desperate hope you will break even.

So I bought more at 8p.

There was a glimmer of hope, and they went to 10p. If they could just creep up a little itty bitty more...

But in early 2002 they sank back to 4p.

Nuts!

Mistake 4 – Denial: the shares will rise!

And then, you've guessed it, I bought some more. (OK, bring on the men with white coats, I'll go quietly.)

Why?

Because of bid rumours!

Sadly, 'bid rumours' do not often come true. Always take bid rumours with a pinch of salt. Of course I really wanted to believe those rumours...

Mistake 5 – Don't get emotionally involved

I found myself going to Coffee Republic more and more. And drinking two or three coffees each visit. Hey, whatever it takes – these guys needed help!

I was the Totally-Hyper-Naked-Trader – unable to sleep at night because of all the caffeine!

In the end I sold for 2.75p, taking a total loss of £8,000.

With the benefit of hindsight

It was a painful time, but I learned an awful lot of lessons from that experience.

 Note The overriding lesson was not to get into that situation (of carrying a big loss) in the first place. Once you get down there, you start looking for reasons to justify yourself, and you make all the wrong decisions.

It's amazing how this, my biggest mistake, has eventually paid itself back, as I now avoid the type of mistakes that led to my loss.

And the main thing is that I've been getting plenty of sleep!

Another of my mistakes

There's nothing worse than holding a share and suddenly you find they are 'suspended'. And what's worse, you see the words 'into administration' in a statement issued the next day. You realise the shares you'd bought are probably worth nothing. Yes – you've lost every penny you put in.

It happened to me when I first started trading. I think it was in 1995, when I held shares in a company called Waterglade which suddenly went bust.

One resolution I made then was it was *never* going to happen to me again. You have no one else but yourself to blame if you're in a share that goes bust. Because, believe me, shares don't just go bust without any warning at all. There are always plenty of signs. It usually starts with a profit warning, then another one, then the company starts talking about 'breaching banking covenants'.

So why do investors end up holding onto companies that go bust, or even in many cases actually buying the company's shares just a few days before the end or even on the day itself?

Look, sorry to have to be basic here, but it's because: *they're greedy idiots*! I was a greedy idiot myself back in 1995.

Courts

The best example I can give which is very recent is Courts, the furniture retailer. I'm sure you all know the story as it ended up on the news – it went bust. (Remember 'Courts you can!', the TV ad with Brucie?)

Yet despite news stories everywhere warning that Courts was in breach of banking covenants, people were *still* buying shares on the very morning the shares were suspended.

And lots of people too. Some in big amounts.

Why were they buying the shares?

They were gambling that the banks wouldn't pull the plug, but it was far too big a gamble to take, and they paid for it by probably losing all their money. As I say, greedy idiots!

The problem is people often think they're getting a bargain and buying a share at a 'basement price'. Half the time they don't even bother looking at the news behind the shares. They just see a share tumbling so buy in the hope of a quick bounce.

They may win sometimes, but I doubt they will over time. It's all gambling and not investing. Investing takes time and effort.

So, how do you avoid buying a company that might go bust on you?

It's simple, do not buy shares:

- That are in trouble with their banks.
- If the words 'banking covenants' are mentioned anywhere in any statement.
- If there is talk about bank facilities being renegotiated.
- If there is mention of re-capitalisation or a dilution of shareholder assets.

So go out there if you want and gamble on these types of companies, but if you buy into them, prepare, as Anne Robinson points out, "to leave with nothing!"

Real traders reveal disaster stories

I thought new investors could learn an awful lot from other people's experiences as well as mine. So, this section contains lots of good advice – from traders and investors who have made big mistakes.

The tales that follow should be carefully read. It seems to me that new investors coming to the market nearly always make the same mistakes as those before them. The great thing is you can read these tales and it has *not* happened to you...yet! Make sure it doesn't.

All the stories below are from real people and these events really took place. Each story has a moral to it, and I've summarised at the end of each story the lessons that can be learned.

Traders tale #1 – Dodgy brokers

The first tale is from Vanessa. She lost a huge amount of money: £500,000. I think it's very brave of her to reveal what happened.

For legal reasons I can't name the broker she used that forms part of the story, So the broker is referred to as 'Broker X'.

"Like many in 2000, I was fairly new to the trading game. I had my first computer, a dial up modem connection and had just found out what the internet was all about. I already had a small portfolio of things like BA, BG, M&S, and a couple of smaller stocks built up over a few years worth about £10,000. I didn't really trade frequently, just tried to invest any spare cash in the markets from time to time in interesting things that I read about and did a little bit of basic research into.

That was until I got a letter from a broker offering me some research and advice on a couple of the smaller stocks that I owned. I was, of course, curious and I ended up having an account with them, a very generous trading limit, and phone calls from them on a very regular basis offering me stock in very small companies at cheaper than market price.

I have to admit to finding it difficult to say no, as I felt that by refusing I would be excluded from information on other things that the broker knew about companies. I tried to buy very small quantities but invariably my broker would say it would not be worth it to buy such a few so I followed his advice.

One share they offered me was at a price lower than the market selling price at the time, but they said I could only buy it on the understanding I could not resell it straight away. Of course I played ball.

On another occasion I decided to buy some shares in Microsoft, and mistakenly asked the broker to purchase 1,000 instead of 100. Now at $54 a share this was a large amount of money. Luckily for me they went up $3 that day, so we sold the excess 900 for a profit.

However, being a conscientious client I had already sent them the money for the 1,000, so three days later there was a large cash balance on my account. No prize for guessing what happened next...they suggested I bought some more small penny shares! I did – what a mug.

Of course, these small shares were not the only things I bought through Broker X. I had been invited to their smart offices and taken out to lunches, so I assumed they had a good reputation and knew what they were doing.

The next big mistake came from me striking up a friendship with another client of Broker X. This happened by chance. Broker X had mistakenly sent one of my contract notes to someone else and this someone else wrote me a very nice letter saying would I like to ring her for a chat sometime.

Whether there was any hidden agenda in this I never knew, but she seemed to be very friendly with a certain tipster. She used to ring me most mornings with "information and rumours". She referred to the tipster as "God" and I too believed this was straight from the horse's mouth.

I think the lesson to be learned from the above is never rely on anyone else's judgement. Doing your own homework is imperative. By the end of 2001 I had lost about £500,000."

There are some big lessons to learn from Vanessa's story.

- Do not buy shares offered to you by anyone, especially at a lower price than the prevailing market price.

If someone is offering you something for nothing, what's in it for them?

- A 'broker' is not necessarily someone to trust! Don't trust someone because they seem plausible and wear a smart suit.

Treat all 'inside information' with suspicion.

Traders tale #2 – Tips from friends

Richard got very excited when he got what he thought was a great tip...

"A very good friend of mine, who works in a pub just on the outskirts of Southampton, rang me to say he had a BT employee in for a pint who told him that: 'Marconi were just about to announce a multi-billion pound contract with BT and the shares should rocket'.

I was immediately excited and looking to open a long spread bet. I asked him when this was likely to be announced, so I could decide whether to do a March or June contract, and he said that the announcement would be made within the next couple of weeks.

On the Monday morning, I watched the March contract go up, and it eventually finished up about twelve points higher.

On the Tuesday, I went long at 692.82 at £10 per point and by the close of play it was at 696.86, giving me an immediate profit of £40.05.

The next day it closed at 722.35, my profit now was £295.30.

By Friday, I was back down to £40.40 profit. But by Wednesday of the next week, I was up £417.35, and by the end of the week, my profit was down slightly at £385.25.

So by the end of nine days, I was ahead by the above figure and I should have been grateful and taken my profit, but no, then the rot set in!

By the time my March contract was about to expire, I was down £843.20!!!!

The announcement never came, and I learnt a very expensive lesson of never to listen to gossip or even tips, from wherever. And if you are fortunate enough to make a profit, bearing in mind I was doing this strictly short-term, take the profit and be grateful, not greedy."

So Richard's story teaches us:

- Don't buy on a tip from a friend.
- Don't take heed of tittle-tattle.
- Spread betting should be short-term – take profits!

Traders tale #3 – Experts in the media

Here's a story from Iain, regarding shares he bought on press speculation.

"I went and bought some Marks & Spencer shares following some positive mutterings in the press. I imagined I could make a quick buck.

About three months later, the price tumbled and Britain's favourite retailer lost about 40% of its value. So much for press 'advice'.

About a month later, the Sema share price crashed and, unlike M&S, I knew this company quite well. I had a lot of friends who worked there. They were highly skilled, happy and productive people, and the company had loads of long-term telecoms and IT contracts.

I had been watching its price daily for months, and its crash from £9 to £2 something seemed only to be explained by the technology bubble bursting – nothing specific to the company itself.

As much as I didn't like to sell M&S for a loss, I wanted to make my money back so sold the lot and invested all I could in Sema at £2.40 a share. A few weeks later, Schlumberger launched a takeover bid and I earned a nice £4.90 a share.

I'm obviously not recommending my random investing style but I am trying to point out that knowing a company first-hand can be far more insightful than information from press 'experts' – whom a lot of the public listen to."

Interesting one!

I agree wholeheartedly with the M&S story. You have to be careful with what you read in the press. It often turns out to be untrue gossip.

Iain made up for it by having a bit of useful knowledge.

So this story says:

- Don't believe press speculation.
- Don't buy on media 'mutterings'.
- Do use knowledge of a company.

Traders tale #4 – Diversification

Philip says he learned the hard way the ups and downs of share dealing.

"It hurts me to tell this story but it happened and it's made me a better trader than if it hadn't. I guess I'm not alone.

Back in the heady days of the late 1990s, I was totally into technology stocks. Not because it was fashionable, but because, with a background in the software industry, I could understand what they did. I was following Jim Slater's axiom in his book, *The Zulu Principle*, where he advocated specialising in a narrow area and getting to know it inside out.

I was lucky I got out more or less at the top of the market in March 2000, with large profits and an even larger ego.

Then the bubble burst and I was left in cash with nowhere to go. I was so conditioned to technology that I couldn't bring myself to buy into old market stocks, even though some were offering huge yields and were making decent earnings.

So I sat on my hands through the early summer while the pundits argued whether the tech stock market would bounce back or not.

This was boring, and so trawling the ADVFN bulletin board one day, I came across a small Manchester based company called Knowledge Management Software, which were heralded as major competitors to Autonomy in the emerging knowledge management market.

I researched the company and talked to the directors, who were bullish in the extreme. I can remember one telling me that he was going to make his fortune in the next five years and then buy a Pacific island with the proceeds. He told me that the shares, then trading around 170p, would go to 450p in the next two years, and he had a lot of them. Maybe that should have put me off, but it didn't; and, to be fair, he wasn't trying to ramp them. He could see the potential for KMS and was excited by it.

I discussed KMS further with some highly knowledgeable and like-minded people on the ADVFN BB, and on 21st June 2000, I bought £10,000 worth of shares at 180p.

Sure enough, within ten days the price had climbed to 197p, and greed kicked in. Maybe I could buy an island too. I went for broke (unfortunate phrase) and bought another 45,000 shares bringing my holding to just over £100,000.

I was now, in my eyes, a major shareholder and KMS in part belonged to me. I identified with the company and this psychological feeling backfired on me later on.

However, at first all went well. The bursting of the tech bubble in March was history, as this software stock rose to 236p by early September and my £100,000 was already worth £120,000 within a couple of months.

Then things started to go pear-shaped.

Nervousness in the market hit tech stocks as a whole in the late Autumn, and prices began heading south. To protect my investment back in June, I had set a stop loss at 150p and had never bothered to move it up behind the price.

In mid November, KMS was sliding towards the stop loss, and I was petrified in fear and disbelief. I knew I should sell if it broke through.

In truth, I should have sold ages before, but wasn't this 'my company' and I'd only owned it for a few months. How could I bale out so soon, even if my original £100,000 was now only worth around £76,000?

Luckily, I came to my senses at 147p and tried to sell the lot on 22nd November. But that's where the normal market size problem hit me and I could only unload 20,000 of the 50,000 shares I was holding. This made matters psychologically worse as, instead of selling the rest next day, I persuaded myself to hold them a little longer as they were bound to recover.

They didn't.

I finally unloaded the remaining 30,000 shares in 10,000 tranches as the price slid down to 118p by the beginning of December, giving me a total loss of over £33,000.

It could have been worse. KMS eventually went into liquidation and I could have lost the lot. But seldom (or is it?) have so many basic mistakes been made in a single trade by someone who had been trading fairly successfully for over five years."

Phillip neatly sums up his mistakes:

- Don't put all your eggs in one basket; someone may kick the basket.
- Always buy a share, never a company; you are not an owner.
- Believe nobody – if a proposition is too good to be true, it's probably false.
- Use a stop loss. Move it up behind a rising price, and use it ruthlessly when things go wrong.
- Be wary of building positions in small companies above their normal market size.
- Recognise greed and fear and cross the street to avoid them.

Traders tale #5 – Tips and gambling

Steve has a salutary tale regarding tipsters.

"Three or four years ago I decided that I would make my fortune through shares. How difficult could it be?

So I started out with £1,000 and decided upon buying about 300 shares in Northern Rock at 296p. They quickly rose to 445p and I sold to make a nice profit of about £400. Nice start, I thought and it convinced me that I was a trading genius!

But the first lesson was to come.

I now had about £1,350 to invest, but in what? I decided on Vodafone at 229p, as they were tipped in a newspaper; and a £500 subscription in the new to be floated Orange, as I had an Orange phone at that time. I made £16 profit on the Orange shares, and watched the Vodafone shares fall. And fall. And fall...... I sold very recently at 132p. The Vodafone money was to give me my biggest lesson: never follow tips!

I was watching *Working Lunch* on BBC2 one day and an apparent expert was explaining how he couldn't understand how Baltimore Technology had plummeted from 220p since he tipped them on his last appearance on the show to about 90p. They must be a bargain now, he implied.

So my £500 went into Baltimore at 88p, and I waited for my money to roll in.

Up went the price... 95p... easy. Then one day it dropped to 60p. I panicked, but held on. Then another sudden drop to 40p – it was collapsing!

I eventually got £18 for my holding a few months ago. I just kept thinking that one day they would go back up. Of course, as I now realise, there were many better shares I could have got into if I had taken my losses and run, but I was used to Baltimore. I knew where I was with them, even though I didn't like it there.

I have made some small profits and losses since, but have not been afraid to get out. I am intending to follow my own research in future.

So, armed with this, together with what I have learned from you and other sources in recent years, I am starting again. I am very much small scale, too small really, but I enjoy it and I can afford a small flutter!

The analogy with gambling is that I wonder how many gamblers started out with a big win and got suckered into thinking it was easy? I do get a gambling type buzz out of buying a new share. It is exciting. Selling at a loss is like backing a losing horse. Making a profit like picking a winner. But how I wish I had got a better price on Northern Rock, or that the race was still running. Or are the lessons I have learnt by making mistakes far more valuable? Time will tell, but I hope the lessons are worth it."

Well, plenty of points to dwell on in that story from Steve! Including:

- Beware the smooth-talking TV pundits.
- Don't let one good trade make you overconfident.
- Cut falling shares quickly.
- Do your own research.
- Watch out for the gambling buzz.

Traders tale #6 – Trading on credit

And now a real horror story from Jeff of Wapping.

> "I was in all sorts of credit card trouble and decided I had nothing to lose in taking out a £10,000 loan and playing the markets.
>
> I knew nothing whatsoever about shares, but bought the usual magazines and followed the tips. My portfolio read like a who's who in crap shares – they all died. My worst was Patsystems. I kept buying all the way down from 130p and sold at 8p.
>
> I was unlucky and even bought some shares just before 9/11. I just kept following tips and refused to sell. I lost the whole lot pretty much. I couldn't tell my wife, and the trading made me very depressed.
>
> There is a happy end to my story though. I did eventually stop trading – or gambling, which is what it really was."

Very important lessons from this story:

- Don't borrow money to trade with.
- Never trade on credit given by brokers.
- Don't trade with money you can't afford to lose.

Traders tale #7 – Broker's credit

On a similar theme, this tale from Robert.

> "When I first started trading I had about £2,000 to play around with. But the website I deal through gave me a £10,000 credit limit until the settlement date, which, in this case, was ten days.
>
> Anyway, I was convinced a share would rise by 10% at least, and so stuck all £10,000 on it, with the intention of selling before the settlement date. It went down quite a lot, and I ended up losing my original £2,000 plus nearly an extra £1,000 of my student loan. Which wasn't too good. But I learned and haven't done it again."

Yes, watch out. Some brokers will give what amounts to credit for ten days, which means you could buy shares and not stump up the cash, with the intention of making a quick buck.

The usual advice holds true: if you're not playing with your own money that you can afford to lose, it's too risky.

Traders tale #8 – Sector knowledge

Phil has an interesting perspective.

> "Any new investor looking for a stock to invest in, should initially look at the companies related to their normal line of work. The reason being: you best know the sector you're working in. You'll have some knowledge of rival companies and their performance, and, as an offshoot, you'll also have some knowledge of your customers' companies.
>
> As an example, I used to work in the IT sector, writing software for the life & pension industry. This meant that I knew of rival companies such as Misys. But it also brought companies like Aviva and Prudential into the picture.
>
> I knew that the life & pension industry had been on the decline for the past three years leading up to 03/04 tax year. With a better economic outlook for 03/04, I traded in Aviva and Prudential because their shares were undervalued. As a result, I made over £4,000 profit. It might not be much compared to seasoned traders, but a profit is a profit."

Some good advice there from Phil. Use the knowledge you have if it gains you an edge.

Traders tale #9 – Stop losses

This tale from Andrew.

> "One share springs to mind, called Minmet. I first came across it on a website where it was getting pumped and pumped.
>
> Being the ignorant trader that I was I took the plunge, buying at prices up to 46p.
>
> From there it was all one way. And now (three years after the purchase), the shares continue to languish below 5p.
>
> The loss is there for all to see, and the lesson learnt. The mistake I made was not to apply a stop loss. And also to believe the tales that Minmet's fall was solely due to 'de-rampers' and that the weakness was a mere temporary blip.
>
> One becomes emotionally attached to the company, and therefore blind to the reality that the price was falling and falling. Despite plenty of evidence to the contrary, I chose to believe the rampers that all was well and we'd be millionaires.
>
> I've now sold out (can't bring myself to say the price). But I now know that stop loss is king, unless you truly believe in the share."

This story really sums it up. Make a stop loss and stick to it. He lost a lot of money by sticking to Minmet even though it kept going down.

Traders tale #10 – Greed

Matthew learned a big lesson when he was only 17.

> "I was only 17. My dad bought me some shares from savings I had in a post office account. The company was VideoLogic. After buying them, they went down. But my dad said, hold on, and they soon increased and changed their name to Imagination Technology. They flew, and over the next year or so I was well up. I'd bought 3,000 shares for 66p and sold them near £4.00. Lovely.
>
> Then towards the end of 1999, I read the City Slickers in the *Daily Mirror.* They tipped Amstrad at around £2.20, saying that the year ahead was going to be amazing and they were launching a new product. I eventually got in at £2.88, piling in all of my profits from Imagination.
>
> Amstrad kept going up. I thought they were going to £10 and not a penny less, because I wanted them to, and if anyone said anything different, I would tell them to shut up. I was greedy and only wanted to believe they were heading for £10 because it would make me richer.
>
> I held 4,000 shares, and if the shares hit £10, I would have £40,000. I wanted that £40,000. It came to the end of March, the day before they launched their emailer, they hit £6.00. The day of the launch the City Slickers said they were going into orbit.
>
> But soon after the shares went down £1.00. And then the whole market started to slide. Looking back it was the start of it all.
>
> The shares continued to slide. I didn't sell because I wanted them to go up further. I didn't want to admit that I was wrong, or that I had believed professionals that had turned out to be wrong.
>
> I just didn't know what to do. My father was as stumped as me.
>
> I ended up selling them quite cheap, around a quid. I don't buy many shares now."

Well, at least Matthew learned his lesson early on in life. To summarise:

- Don't be too greedy.
- Think about selling shares after a 20% gain.
- Beware of bandwagons.

Traders tale #11 – Selling shares

The next few pages of *The Naked Trader* is all about one small email that arrived one day. The mail is short and sweet, but I reckon it's one of the most interesting I've ever received.

After reading it you may think: "What's he on about? What's the big deal about it?"

The big deal, my friends, is this short letter sums up the typical 'fear and greed' mentality which stops investors from selling shares that should be sold.

So, without further ado, here is the letter from Adrian:

> "I've been a reader of your site for well over a year now and this is the first time I've decided to drop you a line.
>
> I thought I'd get your views about my share trading strategy. I bought Marconi at about £4 and just sat and watched them go down to nothing. From £10,000 to £3. Plus a couple of warrants – and I don't even know what they are.
>
> I bought 20,000 Retail Decisions for 4.5p and of course today they are about 28p – a profit of some £4,800. But, for some reason if they start to drift lower, I will probably just sit there and watch them go lower and lower. Why am I seemingly incapable of selling them for a profit?
>
> Maybe it's greed or I suppose it could be that I'm very inexperienced with shares generally."

Adrian has been going through the teething stage that all new investors face. That is, it's easy to buy shares, but not so easy to sell.

That's the fear and greed mentality.

- The inability to sell Marconi was **fear**. Fear that if he sold and took a loss, the shares would immediately rebound and he would be kicking himself.

- The **greed** was Retail Decisions. He was making a great profit and couldn't bear to sell the shares in case they went up more.

It's quite obvious to me Marconi should have been sold at £3.50 (using a stop loss) and Retail Decisions should be sold now! A profit of £4,800 – take the damn thing!

But selling a share is the hardest thing to do.

- Selling one that's turning into a big **loser** is tough because a paper loss becomes a reality.

- Selling a good **winner** is tough because you might be selling it too early.

Look, the answer is blindingly obvious. If wondering whether to sell a share is keeping you up at night, sell the damn thing. There are thousands of shares out there – take the profit or loss and move right along. Just think how many months of anxiety Adrian would have saved himself if he'd sold Marconi and Retail Decisions.

And now, Adrian, here's a secret. I bought Retail Decisions too, for 7p, and sold it far too early at 18p. It's 28p now.

Do I care?

Not in the slightest. I made a profit of around £6,000. That's lovely. So, if I'd stuck around a bit more I'd have made more, but so what? I've made more with the money in other shares.

There probably is another answer for Adrian. Sell half of Retail Decisions. That way you've taken some of your profits and are still hanging onto some of the shares.

But that strategy doesn't work so well with shares on the way down. The whole lot of Marconi should have been sold.

So, when you're sweating over whether to sell a share that's hit a stop loss, or is giving you a big win... just sell! You'll feel a lot better and quite pleased with yourself. Now go use the money somewhere else.

Other views

Adrian's letter is so important that I feel I should share other people's views on it.

I got some mails after I published Adrian's letter so here are some of the best ones giving alternative replies to my (perhaps more gung-ho) views.

One reader, Alan, suggested:

> "Maybe Adrian should try staggering his sales. If he sold half of his Retail Decisions once it slipped a bit, maybe he'd then find it easier to sell the other half if it slipped a bit more.
>
> He thinks he may be 'greedy'. Well, we all want to make money, so we're all greedy! But perhaps his real problem is he doesn't suffer from enough fear. By contrast, I am too nervous an investor, so (for instance) I think the question you have to ask yourself, is why you bought the share in the first place.
>
> Was it for the dividend yield, value fundamentals, or just a punt? I guess the punt is more difficult to guage as normally you're following a crowd and if the news is in the price, exit.
>
> I personally suffer the opposite of Adrian's problem, I sell too quickly!"

Now, another view on Adrian's dilemma from Steve:

> "So many people spend all their energies trying to figure which share to buy, whereas I have found the most difficult thing to learn is when to sell.
>
> We have all heard that we shouldn't get attached to a share. But how do you not get attached? When we first start investing, we spend a lot of time researching a share and only buy once we know it is a winner, such that when it does fall we impersonate the deer in the headlights and stand gawking helpless while it falls.
>
> I think the answer comes with experience. Learning to master the ego: that it is okay to make a mistake and not to take it personally when the market turns against us. We have all heard stories about people that sold a share and it went on to multi-bag. So what? A profit is a profit.
>
> We have all heard that the greatest investors in the world (Buffett, Munger, Legg, Mason, Slater, O'Neill) will always buy a share and hold it through the ups and downs for as long as 30 years. Buffett said that if you do not have the stomach to see your share fall 50%, then you should not be in this game.
>
> I say rubbish! Everybody is different.
>
> If I had Buffett's billions I would also trade the way he does – buy Coca-Cola and wait 30 years for it to make me many zeros while I lived off the divi's.
>
> I think the most important thing is to protect your capital. Never be afraid to take a loss.
>
> Make sure you have enough powder to take on the next trade."

And a final view on Adrian's letter from Keith:

> "I think you have to train your mind to liking and accepting small losses. They are part of the business. I just accept losses as a business cost (i.e. as an employee or two's wages). So Adrian should have sold Marconi – easy. Once losses are fully accepted, they are easy to take.
>
> As for Retail Decisions, that's harder to weigh up. Sometimes it's good to hang on to winners. Adrian needs to make a judgement now on whether shares in Retail Decisions are now overvalued after the huge rise."

Some interesting replies!

I agree that the decision to sell Marconi is easier than the thought of selling the winner. I often hang on to winners for ages. But a profit of more than four times – I think that needs to be bagged.

The main point I reiterate is, if fear and greed over a particular share is eating away at you, sell. You'll feel better and end up trading better because you will be spending your time in a more constructive way.

Traders tales' conclusion

I'd like to thank everyone who submitted stories for the book. These were the pick but there were many other horror stories.

Fear and greed: both these emotions shine through many of these stories.

Most of the contributors simply held onto shares for too long, and got greedier as they went up. Many got more fearful as they went down, but simply couldn't bring themselves to sell.

Perhaps all these stories can be neatly summarised by saying: if in doubt, get out!!

For those new to the market, I hope the stories will make you think about the shares you've bought and will make you take action when things start to go wrong.

Make sure *you* will never have to send me a story like any of the above!

11

What NOT To Buy

You may have seen the show *What Not To Wear*. People who've been dressing badly for years are shown what they should be wearing. It's not much different to shares. Investors start off buying one kind of share and find they can't stop or change their habits.

I feel this chapter may be the most important of the whole book. After all, if you can avoid buying the shares you shouldn't touch with a bargepole, you'll avoid making big losses that drag down your portfolio.

So I'm going to spend some time discussing the types of shares you should take off your monitor screen right now!

Boys with toys

If you're a female reading this book, you'll know what I mean. Boys love toys! That is: gadgets, technology, Star Trek type wizardry, computer games, new computer software, mobile phone add ons – you know what I'm talking about.

And because boys love those toys, when boys look for shares, they immediately get drawn to companies that make the toys. There is a rationale behind it in their minds. The company that makes the gadget is going to go up in value twenty times because everyone is going to use the toy they are developing!

This was the reason why so many of this type of investor lost money in the year 2000. They'd all bought into tech companies. And look what happened! Most of them went tits up (apologies to the girls). Or, at least, they lost huge percentages of their original values.

But lessons haven't been learned and investors still buy into tech companies with one or two products that may end up being a toy that's used in every household. Unfortunately nine times out of ten a new technology struggles, time moves on and it becomes obsolete, or it simply doesn't become a viable toy. I'm afraid there are literally dozens of these types of companies – and I can promise that boys will continue to buy them in the hope of that elusive big share win.

And I should know!

In 1999, tech stocks were all the rage. I did very well out of them – and, with more luck than skill, managed to sell out before the tech bubble burst in 2000.

I bought Scoot.com in 1999. I was seduced by the story. All Scoot really was, was an internet version of the yellow pages. Ahh, but here was the exciting toy thing – and what a fun story this was to whisper to other boys – you see, Scoot had teamed up with the mobile phone companies. So, say you were in a street and you wanted to find out how to get to the nearest dry cleaners, Scoot would tell you using your mobile phone screen.

How exciting was that!

I bought Scoot at 40p and made a fortune as I sold out at 250p. In reality, the shares weren't worth 40p – ever! In fact they ended up pretty much going out of business by 2001.

I bought other tech companies too, and again I managed to sell out near the right time. Let me see, there were so many.

There was one called Parthus. Now this was *really* exciting. You see, its technology let you see exactly where you were using your mobile. So, say you had a child and they had a mobile, you could see where they were. Sounds great, but no one really wanted it.

Boys also like to gossip. There's nothing better than being into one of the toy shares, then telling your mates about it and getting them to buy in!

There are still plenty of tech favourites around today. They don't make a profit, usually only have one or two products and they often have debt, yet the share is rated quite highly, mainly on hope.

Despite the 2000 slump in tech shares and all the money lost, boys continue to pump money into these companies today.

Let me name a few of the boys' toys current favourite toy shares that I steer clear of.

- **NXT:** a real darling of the tech boom – it makes flat speakers. Over the years the company continues to make losses, but the flat speaker story just runs and runs – and seems irresistible!

- **Tadpole Technology:** the small punters' favourite share for as many years as I can remember. I've never understood what they do and I don't think their shareholders do either. The share price has occasional rises when it announces an exciting new development. But these never come to anything and the shares slump back. Investors just like the name I guess.

- **Trafficmaster:** develops telematics. ('Telematics' anyone? No idea what it is, but it sounds cool.) Beloved of tipsters and share punters for a long time. The shares go down mainly, with a bit of up to keep the boys happy occasionally, but as for profits, they never seem to get a mention.

- **Motion Media (now called Scotty):** this one is in the videophone market. Wow – videophones! Sexy – big S. Only problem is, no one seems to want a videophone. Of course, it's a great sounding story so it's another one loved by tipsters and makes for great newspaper articles.

There are plenty more. These shares are nothing more than a gamble, and a poor one at that.

While, occasionally, a boy buying a toy share might make a bit of money catching it at the right time, generally they are the way to the poor house.

> **Note**
>
> Naked Trader says: throw those toys out of the pram!

AIM/Ofex shares

This particular one isn't going to make me very popular with the lads.

Share punters love AIM stocks, but I'm not so keen. The bulletin boards buzz daily with gossip about the next AIM company to strike it big.

AIM stands for Alternative Investment Market. Or as I call it: Absolute Investment Mistake.

It's a junior market and not as highly regulated as the main market. It's (generally) full of tiny companies that could come to something, but more likely won't. It's far cheaper to list on AIM, and the listing regulations are fairly relaxed, so companies that aren't worth much but want a listing can go public.

I suspect among readers this will be my most controversial What Not To Buy.

When you first start investing you will be bombarded with tip sheets and these tip sheets normally focus on AIM stocks. Don't fall for it.

Why?

Because buying these shares is gambling, not investing. Now, I don't completely rule out buying an AIM share if perhaps you have been trading for a couple of years, you're experienced and you want a little gamble. Fine. I do, very occasionally, buy one myself, but for me it's fun money only.

But for beginners: please steer clear!

This is because AIM shares often have wide spreads, they can be hard to sell and they're extremely volatile. Many of the companies are hard to value and so the share prices can leap around. You're guessing and the market makers are guessing. Also, you are at the complete mercy of the market makers who will be ruthless.

Some companies on AIM do very well. And it is possible to make a mint if you manage to get the right one. But you're much more likely to come a cropper.

> AIM stands for Alternative Investment Market. Or as I call it: Absolute Investment Mistake.

So, ignore the tipsters, the bulletin boards and anyone else – and give AIM shares a miss.

I would in fairness point out that the, say, top ten AIM shares, have reasonable market caps and could be tradable.

Ofex shares are even worse. They are even more illiquid and harder to deal in.

Note

Naked Trader says: beginner 'glasshoppers' should stick to the main market.

Tiny market caps

Don't buy shares with a market cap of less than £15 million.

It might sound tempting to buy a company with, say a market cap of £4 million. That's because you want to delude yourself the company could really find its feet and suddenly quadruple its market cap, and you'll be in the money.

The fact is it is highly unlikely, and it's much more likely you are buying a stinker.

Note

Naked Trader says: avoid the small fish.

Loss-makers

There simply is no point buying shares that make a big loss. Why bother when you can buy a decent profit-making company?

My only exception to this rule is if the company has stated it's about to swing into profit from making losses. Or if losses were reported last time because of an exceptional hit – perhaps the company closed a loss-making division.

The trouble with loss-making companies, is despite often confident statements from management, once you're losing money it can be tough to swing into profit.

So if you see it's losing money – why bother?

Note

Naked Trader says: become one with profits.

Super spreads

As mentioned already, you must check the share price spread. That's the difference between the buying price and the selling price.

However enthusiastic you feel about a company, if the spread is much more than 5%, think carefully before you buy. Remember, if the spread is 10% you've already lost a massive 10% of your money just by buying it.

A big spread is telling you that the market makers believe the share is difficult to trade.

Note

Naked Trader says: when it comes to spreads: think thin.

52 week chart breakdowns

It's always worth looking at the chart of a share before you buy. However keen you are, have a good look at the chart for the last year. If the share price is starting to drift below the price the share was a year ago, give it a miss.

It could mean there is trouble ahead.

Note

Naked Trader says: the way to true gains is not down.

Challenging shares

Don't buy any shares which have the word 'challenging' in any part of the company's last statement!

This is extra important and I've already explained this.

Note

Naked Trader says: challenging is just too challenging in the stock market.

Unexplainable companies

Okay, so you like this company. It seems to fit most of the criteria that I keep banging on about in this book. But whenever you're thinking about buying a company you need to ask yourself an important question.

What does it do?

If a friend asks you that, and you can't answer briefly and simply, you really should not be buying it.

For example, I can explain in a sentence what all the companies I have holdings in do. As I write, I hold shares in Sondex, which:

> *"supplies the oil industry with drilling tools and logging equipment."*

Better still, if you can add why you think the company's share price will rise.

> *"The oil price is going through the roof and more and more oil companies are buying or renting equipment from Sondex."*

Or my holding in Telecom Plus.

> *"It provides cheap phone calls and energy services using independent distributors."*

Now, if you own any shares, see if you can explain what they do. If you can't, you need to do some more research.

By the way, if you can't work out what they do from reading the company's last statement, try the company's website.

Note

Naked Trader says: listen to the wind when it says, "err, dunno".

Profit warnings

It's crazy to buy into a company that has recently produced a profit warning.

It's more than likely it'll issue another one, and just because its share price has gone down doesn't mean it won't be going down some more!

Why take the risk? A profit warning means the company is in some kind of trouble or having problems. Why get involved on the off chance of a quick bounceback?

I would suggest far from being a buy, a company issuing its first profit warning is more likely a sell and would even make a good 'short' candidate.

Note

Naked Trader says: a profit warning is like a distant rumble of thunder, the storm's a-coming.

Dead cat bounces

Not a very nice phrase is it? Especially as I'm rather fond of cats.

The dead cat bounce means a share that has been hit badly for some reason; it falls sharply and then starts to rise. This rise often tempts investors to pile in. The share may have, gone down, say, 60 points and then is beginning to rise 5 or 6 points.

For some reason, share punters find it hard to resist buying in.

Using bulletin board language.. the share has been 'oversold' and is about to 'bounce back bigtime'. Don't buy, because you'd be buying in on the 'dead cat bounce'.

After you've bought the share, it will carry on going down and the little rise is then known as the dead cat bounce.

Note

Naked Trader says: dead cats *don't* bounce, believe me on this one.

Falling knives

Don't try to catch a falling knife – it's an old stock market cliché, but it is so true.

Don't be tempted to try and buy a share that's just plummeted. This is the stock market here, it is not like going to the sales and picking up a bargain.

I thought I was pretty smart when I first started trading and I thought trying to buy into shares that had just plunged down a lot was a great idea.

Why?

Well, it's obvious! Surely because they've suddenly dropped a lot they must be a bargain, and they're going to go up! Buying shares that have come down a lot appeals to us traders – we start to think about how much money we'll make if the shares go back to their levels of just the previous day.

I remember the first falling knife I tried to catch – a textiles company called Hartstone. This was in the days before you could get prices on the internet. I used to watch the biggest percentage fallers page on Sky Text. I saw Hartstone shares had fallen from 450p to 280p on a profit warning. And they were starting to go back up! Excitedly, I bought some shares at 280p. And what a flipping genius I turned out to be. Within two weeks the shares were at 320p and I had dreams of them going back towards 450p. Needless to say, I'd done zero research. Then suddenly my dreams were shattered, another profit warning was announced and the shares slumped again – to 175p. I ended up getting out at 120p and with a lesson part-learned.

Only part-learned because I still tried to catch a falling knife another three or four times after that.

For some reason, and it doesn't only apply only to me, buying shares that are falling is irresistible. Every single day of the trading year, you can look at ADVFN's list of the top percentage fallers of the day. You will find a share that's down by 20% – and inevitably you can watch as punters pile in to catch that knife.

Note

Naked Trader says: ouch.

Index trades

I'm presuming you're a relative newcomer to the markets. If so, don't get involved with trading indices too early on in your investing life. Indices are things like the FTSE 100, the Dow, etc.

Index trading is very difficult. Indices move very fast and a winning position can turn into a big losing one in just an hour or two.

Say you decide the FTSE is going to go down or up and bet on that happening with a spread bet. The index can move fast and unless you can keep a very close eye on it, you can get in trouble. It is quite compelling. You see the FTSE 100 has fallen 70 points in the day and it's lunchtime. "Well," you muse to yourself, "it can't fall much further. It'll probably go up!" So you take out a daily up bet. But it goes down some more and you get closed out at a loss.

This type of 'investing' is hard – you are, in effect, trying to predict which way 100 shares are going to go!

Avoid it if you are new to the markets, this also applies to betting on all indices like the Dow and the NASDAQ.

Note

Naked Trader says: index trading is like blind knife throwing – not for beginners.

Tipped shares

The Sunday papers tip quite a few shares. If you're new to the markets it's very tempting to get on to your computer first thing on Monday morning and buy the tip as the markets open.

Nooooooooooo!!!!

You did understand that, didn't you? The market makers have already seen you coming and will have you for breakfast.

They will have seen the tip and they know full well that there will be demand for the shares, especially early on in the day. So the swines mark up the share involved before the market opens.

If you go in and buy right away, you'll be buying at an inflated price. Market makers could well add 5% or more to the value of the share. And once they've got you in their clutches, what's the next thing they want you to do? Of course! Panic you into selling them – and that often works.

Using these wily tactics, the market makers will have sold you shares at a high price, and then buy them back off you much lower. The only person who wins...yes, you've guessed it, those dastardly market makers.

The same rule applies to any tipped share. This is where the bulletin boards come in handy. If a share is rising, check carefully it hasn't been tipped and you're not buying into a false rise.

Note

Naked Trader says: nooooooooooo!!!!

12

The Seven Deadly Sins Of Share Trading

I'm not in the slightest bit religious, but I do think there is something in the famous seven deadly sins. The more I looked at these sins, the more I found they related to share dealing. I reckon if you can avoid these sins, you have a better chance of trading profitably.

So here's an idea. Put these deadly sins onto a bit of paper and hang it somewhere near where you trade; every time you make a buy or a sell check you're not committing one of them.

So let's kick off with the number one which is...

Pride

Pride is the 'excessive belief in one's own abilities'. Pride is really deadly. You simply can't afford to have this deadly sin if you're going to trade.

What's so bad about pride?

Pride is going to stop you from selling a share that's going down. You're a proud guy - when you bought at 300p you were certain the share was a good one. You set a stop loss at 270p and it's now 260p. But you go:

"Oh, sod the stop loss! I'm right! It'll go back up. I don't get things wrong. It's those idiotic market makers messing things up. And those that are selling are real idiots. I'm right and everyone else is wrong."

Pride will carry on stopping you from selling the share now - in fact pride may even make you buy more at lower prices... because you were right first time.

The real problem with pride is it'll simply stop you selling something at a loss. I always bang on about cutting your losses early, but those with pride just won't do it. You can't bear the thought of phoning up a broker or a spread firm to close something out at a loss. Your pride just won't be able to stand it. So you'll hold on and on to the share while it sinks.

At the other end of the scale, if things are going well with your trading, pride may make you overconfident and lead you to overtrade... hence the phrase: "Pride comes before a fall."

So I beg you to make me feel proud of you. Bin the pride and keep it out of your trading.

Envy

Envy is the 'desire for others' traits, status, abilities or situation'.

It's a horrible sin. This usually comes about from reading about other people bragging about their trading success on the bulletin boards. Especially bad is when you read about someone buying a share at 2p and getting out at 12p. Or from reading about someone who's made a fortune out of shares. You want to be that person.

What happens is the envy you feel from reading about this kind of success drives you to trade far too much and buy far too risky shares, because you too want to be a success. You'll simply overreach yourself in trying to achieve it. Making money from shares takes time.

So don't be envious of other people's success. For a start they're probably exaggerating their success. Work on an exaggeration factor of about 60% – you know what us blokes are like.

But even if their claims are true, don't try and copy them or put money into the market you can't afford.

Be your own man (or woman). Stay envy and emotion free when trading.

Sloth

'The avoidance of work.'

Oh it's sooo easy to be slothful. Believe me, I have a tendency to be slothful, but not when it comes to buying and selling shares. It's the easiest thing in the world to be slothful about share dealing.

Why do you think there are so many tipsters and tip sheets out there? And why do they make a profit? They get their money from slothful investors who want to slob around and not do any of their own research.

It's much easier just to buy on someone else's tip. How easy is that? Much easier than bothering to read through reports yourself. Or you could just buy any old share you see hyped on the bulletin boards without even bothering to look at any fundamentals. Perhaps just a quick look at the charts to justify to yourself you've done a bit of research.

Stop the sloth!

Research shares properly, concentrate on what you're doing...remember it's your money you're going to be losing. Think carefully and look at a share from and as many angles as you can. Read the company statements and reports. Look at the charts properly. Take your time and put in the work. Now you may start to make money.

I know for a fact one tip sheet has made money for years from investors so slothful that they've even given up investing...but were so lazy they couldn't be bothered to cancel the direct debit!

Sit in front of the TV with a beer for hours in your Y-fronts if you must (or boxers for a trendy young man like me) (who you kidding? – Ed), but I urge you, when it comes to trading, put in the hours.

Greed

'The desire for material gain.'

Well, that definition is certainly right. You wouldn't have bought this book if you weren't a bit greedy and I wouldn't have written it if I wasn't. So that's two of us then. Anyway, I don't believe there's anything wrong with the desire for material gain.

However greed when trading is one of the main failings of investors. And believe me, it is very easy to fall into greedy ways. This usually happens when you've had a good run – a few of your shares have gone up and you feel like you're the master of your domain, king of the hill, top of the heap (is that a song?).

Greed now makes you overreach yourself. You suddenly get greedy and start buying loads of shares with money you haven't got because you want to make more and more money. But what usually happens is over-trading suddenly leads to too many positions being open with the inevitable consequence that profits turn into losses. Then of course pride sets in and you won't cut your losses. (See Pride.)

Greed can also lead you to try and make money too quickly, which leads to a loss of patience which usually means taking on too much risk with the usual dire consequences.

So eat three big pizzas in one go and guzzle ten pints with it if you must, but when it comes to trading, being greedy is a bad move. This brings us nicely onto...

Gluttony

'A desire to consume more than one requires.'

Put another way, this is trading with money you don't have. This is easy to do these days with CFDs, spread betting and credit from brokers.

Companies are very happy to let you buy CFDs and spread bet 'on tick' - or what they call 'margin' trading. That is, they let you buy, say, £1,000 of exposure to a share when you only have to actually put up £100. This leads you to gluttony. You end up spending too much money you don't have.

But if you play with these margined things and go over the top, things can spiral out of control very quickly. You may find you buy more and more CFDs without any thought about whether you can really afford to take out so many positions without putting up the money. If you don't have the money, don't trade using too much margin. Keep the gluttony at bay.

Wrath

F****** b******* s****** and even the occasional c******* if things get really bad.

All investors have shouted rude words at the screen when their investments start to slide.

Frankly, I think this is the least of the deadly sins to worry about. After all, we all get angry about our trades from time to time. And that doesn't really sound like much of a deadly sin, does it?

There is a danger with this deadly sin, though. Wrath is an emotion, and emotion is to be avoided at all costs when dealing in shares.

Wrath is okay unless we let it get the better of us. The best example is getting angry because a share you were keen on is going down. The problem with feeling angry is you then feel the share 'owes you' and you end up buying more to try and break even. Believe me, the chances are you'll feel even more wrathful the day after you bought more and it carries on going down.

Also, don't get angry with others, for example on bulletin boards. Don't slag other people off all the time; it's a waste of time that you could be spending on research.

So, if you feel wrathful, take a break from the screen or go meditate.

Lust

Unbelievably, some investors fall in love with their shares. They really seriously lust after them. It could be the share has a nice name. Two shares that spring to mind that investors kept buying despite falling shares prices are: Tadpole and Wiggins (now Planestation). For some reason known only to themselves investors lusted after these two loss-makers and bought and bought again.

Bulletin board writers roared "Go Wiggy Go!". You can tell from looking around the bulletin boards the lust there is out there for certain shares. And for some strange reason, investors tend to fall in lust with the worst possible shares.

The same case can actually be made even if it's a relatively good share and you've made profits. You've fallen in lust and simply can't sell if it starts to tank.

So don't fall for lust. You're not dating shares – think of them as just acquaintances that can be dumped anytime without worry.

If you're feeling lusty there are plenty of non-share related internet sites out there that can help you. (If you want more information you'll have to call the Naked Trader £10 a minute lustful premium rate phone line.)

13

Buyer Beware!

Why it's a dog eat dog market

This is the chapter telling you to watch out. But that doesn't mean you can skip reading it. There's important stuff here!

There are a lot more stock market losers than winners, and there are people out there who spot newcomers to the market and they want your money. Before you go rushing in to buy shares, remember the world you are going into is cut-throat. And if you follow or listen to the scam merchants, you will be the loser! So this is a very important chapter.

Beware the scam merchants

It sounds horrible, but think of everyone out there in shares land as your enemy unless over time you are convinced otherwise. The friendlier they appear, the more likely it is you will get led up the garden path.

There are many traps awaiting the novice trader. The moment you sign up for internet sites, to find your email inbox and snail mail address start to get bunged up with enticing offers. You may even start to get phone calls. (Your details, of course, are always sold on.)

And, boy, will you get offers!

You'll find everyone out there will want to offer you tips, an amazing trading system and shares at under market price. They'll sell you ways of making money on the markets, ways which really can't lose.

Ignore all offers and concentrate on learning about the markets slowly and cautiously – do not get sidetracked by the easy way out.

Being new, or newish, to the markets, it's only natural you'll want to follow a tipster, a guru or some other mentor. We're a herd animal and so the minute you start trading you'll want to find a 'leader'.

Don't.

However tempting it is, treat all tips, offers of advice, newsletters, phone calls, offers of shares, research documents, share systems and software with extreme suspicion.

Share scams come in various forms and guises. Here are some to watch for:

Phone calls

These often come from America. A plausible sounding bloke opens up with a question like: "You handle your own portfolio, how's it going?" When you mumble something like "it's going ok," he'll start a sales pitch. He has an incredible tech stock that is going to treble in a few weeks and he's offering YOU the chance to get in!

It could be one of a couple of scams.

This bloke will probably claim to be from a broker who can let you have this wonder stock cheaper than the current market price. What it means is he, or even a reputable-sounding broker, has bought a shed load of stock in a crap company and wants to offload some to you at a worse price, thereby making a guaranteed profit.

Or it could be worse; you could send your money off and never see it again!

Alternatively, the call could come from a UK company offering tips or shares at a knockdown price. Again the share is likely to be a small penny share and they are trying to make money out of you in the same way as above.

Note

Ignore all these and just hang up. You are unlikely to get rich quick and more likely to become considerably poorer.

Before hanging up, ask them where they got your phone number and try and get off the list – otherwise, in my experience, you'll be inundated with phone calls.

Newspaper/magazine get rich ads

I'm sure you've seen these. They usually say something like, "Learn stock market secrets...", or "Make £400 a day from home...".

Usually what happens is you get enticed along to a free seminar. The guru will talk about things like spread betting and technical analysis and then spend the rest of the time trying to flog his work manuals, books, and another paid-for seminar or expensive software.

The plain fact is: if it seems too good to be true, it usually is.

It is highly unlikely you'll 'make £400 a day'. The guru will make money out of you by selling you his books, videos and courses. Again, all you have to do is ask yourself: if the guru is such a genius why doesn't he sit at home with his systems, rack up the millions and be happy?

I'm not saying all such systems and all software are no good. I just don't think these are a great way to learn how to make a good start in the stock market.

Note

There's no substitute for learning to do your own research and gradually learning the ins and outs of trading.

Scam summary

- Don't buy shares offered over the phone.
- Be sceptical about get rich ads.
- Software may be an expensive waste of money.
- Don't take the 'easy' way – take time to learn about the market.

Bulletin boards – all the hype!

It can be a lonely business buying and selling shares. But that's where the internet bulletin boards (BBs) come in. They are great fun to read and worth a look if you are researching a particular company.

The four most active biggest BBs are at:

- www.advfn.com (click 'Free BB'),
- www.hemscott.com (click 'Info Exchange')
- www.moneyam.com (click 'Investors' Rooms')
- www.iii.co.uk (click 'Community')

All contributors have chosen a nickname. So you have no idea who they are. If you want to contribute, you just register on the site, pick your nickname and you are away.

On ADVFN and MoneyAM each topic is called a 'thread', and they appear in order of last update.

Hemscott is slightly different. Someone makes a comment and then someone replies to that comment (or not).

BBs are like a big pub where blokes (generally) talk about shares in the same way they talk about football in the pub.

Note

The main rule regarding the BBs is: treat them as light entertainment!

Whatever you do, don't buy something because someone nicknamed 'Saddambinladen' or suchlike says to. Bear in mind that 80% of BB contributors are trying to push the share they've just bought. So treat everything you read with some suspicion.

Ramping

'Rampers' is a term applied to those who continually talk up a share they are holding in the hope others will buy in and so raise the price of the share in question. They then hope to quickly sell in the strength generated and make a profit.

They will say or write anything to make you buy. They will often claim to have inside information or say there's a 'bid coming' or there's an amazing 'chart breakout'. They pick on the smallest shares in the market and make clever remarks about them intended to suck you into buying. Sometimes there is a small gang of people all working together.

They know if they can get 20 or 30 people to buy in after them, they can push a tiny share up by 20% or 30% after they've bought. They get busy selling while those sucked in are buying. So after they've bought their shares in Completely Crap PLC they will get on to the BBs that are most popular and post comments like: 'Crap company is about to treble.' That should be enough to entice you onto the Crap PLC bulletin board, where of course you will be met with a lot of breathless hype.

Once The Crap PLC price has shot up just after those duped have bought in, Crap will issue a statement saying they know of no reason for the share price rise and they are as crap as ever. The price immediately goes back to where it was, the ramp gang are happy with their profit leaving the mugs poorer but probably wiser.

Note

The main lesson here is: don't believe everything you read, especially if comments are made about an illiquid company with a small market cap.

As well as rampers, you also have to look out for the de-rampers!

These actively spread bad information about a company on the BBs. The idea behind this is to worry holders into selling because the de-rampers want the stock to fall – either because they have shorted it, or because they want to buy it back cheaper.

There are also 'rampers' who are very subtle and these are the ones you *really* have to watchout for!

These rampers have reassuring sounding nicknames like 'your mummy' and set themselves up as BB gurus. The title of the thread will be something like 'Mummy's Picks' or 'Superguy's superstocks'. Other investors come onto threads they have set up, and ask for advice or some technical analysis regarding shares they hold.

Again, take what they say with a big pinch of salt. They may not know what they are talking about.

They paste charts onto the threads and then make predictions which all sound very plausible. Some of them are probably genuine people, but some aren't and when it comes to it, they spend time creating their guru status so they can get other people to buy into the, usually very small, companies they are ramping.

Quite often, you suspect they have three or four different nicknames and pretend to be other investors. It might go like this:

CUTEINVESTOR: (who might be Supershares in disguise)

↳ That was a great call you made on Crap PLC well done!! I wondered if you could look at Deep In Debt PLC for me.

SUPERSHARES:

↳ I like the fact DID has come back to test its trendline. It's bounced back to create a very nice handle formation. The longer-term chart shows potential and the indicators are showing green shoots. Base of the cup is 50p and the top is 86p so add 65p onto the lip of the cup and you have 151p which isn't far away from resistance. Looks good to me, imo and dyor.

CUTEINVESTOR:

↳ Thanks Supershares, I think I'll buy some tomorrow!

DELBOY:

↳ I like the DID chart too – Supershares, your call on Crap was excellent!

So what was all that about then?

Well you see how subtle that piece of ramping was. Both Supershares and the others know many people will read the stuff about Deep In Debt PLC. DID is probably a tiny company with a small market size, and just fifteen people buying next morning could push it up a few per cent – Supershares and friends would sell while the last people were buying and take their profits.

Notice all the jargon which sounds quite compelling! They're not even telling people they should buy, it is all so subtle! Even down to the imo (in my opinion) and dyor (do your own research).

That's all subtle ramping.

Note

And don't forget, all those messages could be from the same person.

There are also actual gangs of rampers: a group of people who all get together to push penny shares. It's not at all subtle but it seems to work well, especially on new investors who aren't clued up.

Here's one share a ramping gang managed to raise by a huge percentage.

It's a company called **Zyzygy**. In a few days they got the share from half a pence all the way to 1.75p! That's a big percentage move. Of course the company was never worth more than half a pence.

How did the rampers do it?

They simply blasted every bulletin board they could with messages about how amazing the company was and how everyone would be on a 'ten bagger'. Luckily for them, once the share started its rise it got easier and easier as their audience got greedier and greedier. They could then start messages like "Zyzygy up 15% – plenty more to come, get on now!!".

Zyzygy: January 2003 – August 2005

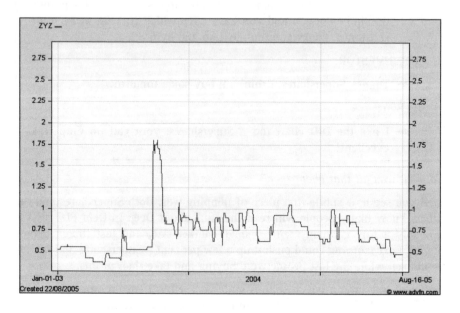

You can see for yourself what happened by looking at the previous chart. That big spike in the price is due to the clever rampers. The poor suckers who bought right at the end of the ramp were the ones who really suffered and they're the ones that really lost. As you can see, after hitting 1.75p the rampers sold out quickly and the share retreated back to its truer level.

Here's one example of a BB comment:

> "Cash shell with very good management.
>
> City rumours state that ZYZ will acquire a suitable business soon.
>
> Do not be left behind when this one shoots through the roof !
>
> FACT: This whole company is worth less than a 3 bedroom semi at the present moment ! EVERY SINGLE BUY of a few hundred pounds MOVES THE SHAREPRICE !
>
> I've just topped up on these, I've been buying for a year now and am confident that the information that my sources have given me will be VERY positive for ZYZ."

Note the 'inside sources' – the hint that the poster knows stuff about the company that will soon turn it into a super company.

But he was right about one thing – every single small buy *did* help to lift the share price – a real rampers' dream! The bulletin board began with "Potential ten bagger – this share will fly!". You can still see it on ADVFN now. Take a look for yourself on the ADVFN BB and see how a small gang managed to push up the price.

Ramps normally come to an end when the company concerned is pretty much forced to issue a statement, which is what Zyzygy did:

> 26th September
>
> Zyzygy Plc
>
> ("Zyzygy or the Company")
>
> The directors of Zyzygy have noted the sharp movement in the Company's share price. Although discussions are taking place with interested parties, none of these have progressed beyond a preliminary stage and, accordingly, the directors are not aware of any reason for this movement.

By the time the company issued this, the rampers had taken their profit. After the statement, the punters who bought in were scrambling to get out...at a loss!

So, unwary investor, beware of these ramps on the BBs. I am sure in time they will try their techniques on Zyzygy again. Expect a share spike any day.

Note Ramps are so easily avoided, simply don't buy tiny illiquid companies. Stick to normal market sizes of at least £2,000 and market caps of more than £20 million.

BBs – The good part

If it seems I'm being negative about bulletin boards, there are loads of positives! If there weren't, I wouldn't have set up my own board on ADVFN.

Sometimes there *is* some decent information to be had. There are times when an investor will phone a company and report what the company told them on the BB.

Some investors cut and paste reports on the company or newspaper comments or articles or reasons why the price is going up or down.

And some posters really *are* well-informed and come up with decent and well worked-out predictions.

Some are just wind-up merchants who don't even trade and just like winding people up. Watch out for posters who can't post during the day. This is a big clue they don't really trade much but want to appear authoritative.

Note If researching a company, it's always worth checking out the BBs because you can get a general feel about the company and some bits and pieces worth noting.

Just be cautious! Particularly if someone urges you to "Fill Ya Boots!".

> **Bulletin board/ramp summary**
>
> - BBs should be used mainly for entertainment purposes.
> - Don't get conned into buying worthless shares.
> - Treat everything you read as suspicious.
> - Beware of the subtle rampers.

Tipsters – the bad

I'm afraid to say the market is littered with a varied assortment of what I can only describe as 'dodgy geezers' wanting to take your money in return for their 'hot tips'. Some will even offer 'free' tips, but of course they will exploit your email address or inundate you with offers of paid for tips.

There are loads of share tipsters around, as you will very quickly find out. They usually charge a fee for access to tips, or they come in the form of a monthly 'newsletter'. Like entertainers, they all have some kind of 'schtick' to pull you in. Some claim to be maverick city insiders. Others to "read the charts and the signals".

Every single tipster will quote what seems like amazing performance figures: "Our tips are up 40% this year!", "Amazing profit every year", "Three penny shares that are about to rocket!" What they don't brag about is the ones they picked that halved in value or even went bust. So you won't see headlines like: "We tipped a share and it went bust."

There'll usually be a list of shares with percentage profits made against each one. Amazingly you'll see hardly any losing shares. Obviously following these geniuses is a licence to print money!

Sadly, their claims are unlikely to be realistic. Some tipsters are very clever and use various manipulation of stats to show performances that generally just aren't true.

Something else you won't find in their claims: all their tips that have gone south or gone bust! You'll only see the winners highlighted and my cat could have picked some of those by sticking her paw at random on the share prices in the *FT*!

Nearly all of the tipping organisations tip very small penny shares. You won't find them tipping many bigger companies. That's because in percentage terms they only have to hit on one or two big winners (out of the dozens of companies they tip).

Here are just some of the ways they create amazing performance figures.

They often use mid prices. Never the real buy and sell prices. With the small company shares they tip, this means they are already up on the percentage game. Let's take an example. A tipster tips a share that is 9p to sell and 10p to buy. So the tipster says his tip is at 9.5p – the mid price. No one can actually buy at this price, but never mind! The tip is published in a tip sheet at the weekend. On Monday, before the market opens, the market makers have seen the tip and raise the price to 10p to sell and 11p to buy (mid price is now 10.5p). Subscribers buy in at 11p, but the tipster can now claim to have profits of an amazing 10 %!! (The difference between his mid price tip at 9.5p, and the new mid price of 10.5p.)

What has actually happened is those who bought the tip are already nursing *losses* of nearly 10%. They've bought in at the real buy price of 11p, but the selling price is only 10p!

What's worse is that the market makers know the mug punters have bought at 11p and during the next few days will drop the price, and those who bought will suffer even worse losses.

The tipster doesn't care: that now goes down as a 10% profit. On the 'table' of winners it will show: tip 9.5p, high 10.5p, +10%!

None of the subscribers could possibly have bought or sold at these prices.

Of course, most of the tipsters tip anything from 50 to 200 companies a year. There's no way subscribers could afford to buy that many of them.

So even when a tipster manages to tip a big winner, chances are the subscriber won't have bought it. It's Sod's Law but they will probably buy the one that's gone bust!

None of it matters because while people are cancelling subscriptions, there are always new mugs ready to start up a subscription.

In particular, tipping publications love direct debit payments. That's because us Brits are so lazy we rarely cancel them, so they carry on taking money off you long after you've tired of losing money!

Tipsters – the good

Okay, of course as with everything there *are* some good tipsters out there. There are probably five or six names that are worth paying attention to. If you can find someone tipping who trades as well, that would be an advantage. Alternatively, someone who perhaps specialises in certain shares, for example, the FTSE 350.

If you don't feel like finding your own shares, how can you find the good tipping services?

The clue is to ask around. Try the bulletin boards, put up a message – is so-and-sos' tipping service any good? Have you made money by following the tips?

Bulletin board writers are notoriously difficult to please, so if you do read plaudits for a tipping service, then maybe, just maybe, you should have a look.

If you do join a tipster service, don't just buy the tipped shares automatically. Do your own research. Look on the tips as a possible basis for further research. Monitor the service carefully and write down the real prices you could have bought or sold at and judge performance yourself.

And whatever you do, don't buy a tip right away. The market makers will have marked up the tips and if you buy right away the price will be far too high. Wait for a few days for the share to settle down.

Note

If you subscribe to tip sheets, you must only use them to help you generate ideas.

The other sort of tips you get are the free ones in investment magazines and newspapers. Again, beware of the market maker mark up – these shares should not be bought right away. Be especially careful of buying tips in the Sunday papers, as on a quiet Monday morning these will already be higher and you will be paying too much.

In addition, remember these tips are being written by journalists. They are probably only on £25k a year. If they were any good at picking shares they'd be trading full-time themselves! They are also under pressure to come up with tips and ideas so they are not necessarily going to be much good.

Tipsters summary

- Beware the performance figures quoted.
- Do you really need a guru?
- Tips are marked up before you can buy.
- Don't sign direct debits to tipping organisations – pay by cheque.

Systems

Everywhere you look in the stock market someone somewhere will be trying to sell you a system.

These people promise you the world: "Spend just five minutes a day and make £2,000 a week", "Our system picks all the trades for you", "Trade from home and make £75,000 a week with no experience".

Just think about it.

Don't you think if the people that came up with the systems had come up with an easy way to make millions they'd keep it to themselves and end up in Barbados sunbathing? Don't be fooled by promises of big profits for no effort, and take anything they say, like their 'record of profits', with a giant pinch of salt.

The only system is to learn about trading slowly but surely through hard work and decent research. You get nothing for nothing. Ignore the ads and bin the junk mail.

Recommended reading

This is discussed in more detail by Kevin Goldstein-Jackson in his fine book *The Astute Private Investor*. His book has many interesting hints and tips and is well worth a read.

14

Spread Betting

Introduction

Spread betting has come a long way since it was devised years ago as a tool to be used by a small bunch of City professionals. It keeps growing in size and is becoming more and more popular. I'm not surprised. Spread betting is easy to understand, in fact these trades are often easier to execute compared to a normal shares account. I use my spread betting account more and more these days.

Spread betting is an important tool and a spread betting account, I feel, is a must-have even for newer investors.

But it's also a dangerous tool. If you consider a normal shares account is a Ford Fiesta, then spread betting is a high-powered Ferrari. If you put your foot down you'll take off too fast, and when it is time to apply the brakes you might be too late to avoid a crash. There are several reasons for this which I will cover shortly.

Generally, I believe spread betting should be thought of for mainly short-term trading. That is, it's not the tool to use to buy a share and expect to hold it for a couple of years. You should be looking at anything from a week to four months maximum.

You should take note that it's called spread 'betting' and not spread 'investing'! But make sure you use spread betting as an investment tool, not a gambling one; although, of course, the odd quick gamble is okay – life is for living!

The mechanics

An attraction of spread betting is that no tax is paid on winnings. That's not bad, is it? But the biggest advantage of spread betting for me is the ability to short stocks. In other words: to make money when shares *fall*.

However, there isn't space here to give a full explanation of spread betting. If you're completely new to this spread betting world, I'd strongly recommend reading *The Beginner's Guide to Financial Spread Betting* by Michelle Baltazar.

In this chapter I'll just focus on a few spread betting topics that I think are important.

First, let's get started with an example.

Trade example

You phone the spread betting company (or use its website) and discover BSkyB is quoted at 500-505 (i.e. 500 to sell, and 505 to buy).

It's very simple:

- You think the shares are going **down** (you want to short them)? Then sell at 500p.
- You think the shares are going **up** (you want to go long)? Then buy at 505p.

In this case, BSkyB shares have gone down recently and you think they will recover. So you buy at 505 for £10 per point.

Note If the BSkyB price goes up 10%, that will be an increase of roughly 50 points, and the trade will make £500. This is equivalent to owning approx 1000 shares in BSkyB (of value £5,000) – where, if the share prices rises 10%, the share value will also increase £500.

If the price rises to 545-550, you've made money. You can close out the position by selling at £10 per point at 545p. You've made 40 points (545-505), which is £400 profit (£10 x 40 points).

Alternatively, you may think BSkyB shares are going to tumble a lot further and you want to make money on a drop. In that case you sell at the sell price of 500p for £10 a point. Three weeks later the price is 450-455. If you'd sold, you'd be in the money! If you sold you would then have to buyback the buy price – in this case 455p – to close out the position.

You've made 45 points (500-455), which is a profit of £450 (£10 x 45 points).

However, if you'd bought the shares at 505p, you'd have to close out at the sell price of 450p. That's a loss of 55 points (505-450) or £550.

When phoning to close out a bet you'd normally tell the dealer it is a *closing trade*.

Are you still with me? No? It took me a while to get my head round it and I have the attention span of a goldfish!

Go get a cup of coffee and go through that example again. It's important to understand it!

If you don't, head for my website www.nakedtrader.co.uk contact me there and I'll be happy to go through this on email.

Do NOT put on a spread bet on unless you fully understand that you buy at one end of a spread and sell at the other!

Net or phone?

Whether you use the net or phone is up to you. I still use the phone 95% of the time for spread betting, even though I use the internet 100% of the time to buy shares in the market with a broker. I find spread betting on the phone fast and easy – a quote in seconds, the trade in seconds and no fiddling around on the computer. Perfect!

Cantor Index has always answered the phone to me in a few seconds, even during busy times, and trades have always been carried out efficiently and courteously.

One issue that comes up time and time again from website readers is: "I can't seem to trade the company you just traded with my spread firm!"

You *can*!

Firms only quote the top 200 or so companies directly on the net. For smaller companies you have to phone for a quote. Generally, the spread firms will allow you to deal in any company as long as their market cap is above £50 million.

Don't expect to be able to take out big positions as the firms are likely to only let you have a stake at the normal market size.

Some of the spread firms have amazing websites with loads of free tools – it's worth shopping around.

Expiry dates

Unlike normal share buying whereby your buy remains a buy forever, unless you decide to sell or, God forbid, your share goes bust, spread trading is different.

When you place a spread bet you need to set an expiry date. Most expiry dates are set at three-monthly intervals – September, December, March and June. The expiry date itself is usually the third Tuesday of the month for shares and the third Friday for indices. However you can set a different time if you want: daily; weekly; fortnightly or monthly.

I usually go for the next quarter, unless it's close to expiry in which case I'd go for the quarter after. The further away the expiry date, the bigger the spread. Unless you're a skilled day trader, I'd avoid the daily expiry.

Rolling over

Expiry dates mean within three months you will *have* to take your profit or loss – not such a bad thing. But you *can* keep hold of the trade by what's called a 'rollover'. Nope, nothing to do with the lottery. A rollover means you close out the current trade, and 'roll' it over to the next quarter. So you basically take your profit or loss and a whole new trade is set up. Unfortunately you have to pay via a new spread, but most firms will give you a decent discount on that.

Personally, I rarely rollover. If you have to rollover it often means a short-term trade that's gone wrong!

Spreads and costs

If you buy shares in the market and it's a FTSE 100 share, the spread will be at most a point or two. But don't be surprised when you call up your spread firm, ask for a spread price and find that it's a lot wider than if you were buying the share normally.

It's not fair to tell the dealer: "You're having a laugh, what's the real spread?"

The spread is wider because that's how the spread firm (generally) makes its profit. Hey, these guys have to make their money too, you know, give them a break.

Referring to the BSkyB example on page 218, where I was quoted 500-505, the quote in the underlying share might have been 500-501 at the time.

"Why bother spread betting," you may cry. "I'd rather take the narrow spread and buy the shares in the normal manner."

But you're forgetting something. You do not have to pay commission to your broker, *and* you don't pay the dreaded stamp duty *and* you don't have to pay capital gains tax on any winnings.

So how do the costs compare between normal trading and spread trading?

It's quite hard to work that one out. Different spread firms charge different spreads at different times. It also depends on how you like to trade.

Let's take the BSkyB example again, and let's try to work out a cost comparison between normal share dealing and spread dealing very roughly.

In this example we will pretend the shares were 500-501 in the normal market and 500-505 in the spread market when the shares were bought.

Then we'll say the shares go up to 549-550 in the normal market and 548-553 in the spread market.

Normal share trade

- Buy 1,000 shares at 501p. Value = £5,010
  Buying costs: broker commission = £12.50; stamp duty = £25.05

- Sell 1,000 shares at 549p. Value = £5,490
  Selling costs: broker commission = £12.50

- Profit = £480. Costs = £50.05

- Net profit = £429.95

Spread trade

- Buy £10 a point at 505p. Sell at 548p. No costs.

- Profit = £430

So, not much in it there – and I reckon generally there is not much in it.

What probably makes it cheaper to use spread betting is if you are a larger trader and you easily make more than £8,500 profit a year (CGT allowance for 2005/2006). Say you'd already used up your capital gains tax allowance. Top-rate taxpayers would have to pay 40% tax on that profit of £480, or a massive £192! In this case, it would be much better to spread bet than buy in the normal market.

I could come up with loads of different examples and each one would throw up a different cost comparison.

For example, Vodaphone, the most actively traded share on the market, would probably be cheaper to spread bet as the spread will be very tight. But a company with a 3-4% spread might be better off being traded elsewhere.

The rule of thumb is: the tighter the spread given by the spread firm, the more cost-effective.

Stop losses

One of the greatest benefits of spread betting is you can set a stop loss.

This means discipline is imposed on you and your trade will be closed out at your stated stop loss. It is much more difficult in the share market.

But there are a few points you should understand.

Let's say you've bought BSkyB at 505p. You decide your stop loss should be about 50 points so you set a stop at 455p. If the share goes below that you'd rather take the loss than rack up any more losses.

There are *two* different types of stop loss:

- **Ordinary stop loss**
  On an ordinary one, the spread firm will try and get you out at the loss, but if the share is moving fast you may end up being closed out at 445p rather than 455p.

- **Guaranteed stop loss**
  A guaranteed one means what it says – you will be closed out at 455p. But a guaranteed stop loss will cost you a bit of extra spread, so your 505p buying price may be adjusted to something like 507p, costing you the equivalent of £20 on your £10 per point buy.

I would say it's generally worth paying the extra spread and getting the guarantee.

Take this example.

You've bought BSkyB at 505p but a week later the company issues an early morning statement. The market doesn't like it and the shares open at 355p.

Under a normal stop loss you will be closed out at 355p – a full 100 points lower than your stop loss. That would cost you £1,000 more (at £10 per point) than if you'd used the guaranteed stop loss of 455p. Because the firm guaranteed you 455p, that's the price you'd get even though the shares had opened at 355p.

Note

Don't forget: when you close out a trade, you must also cancel the stop loss.

One word of warning on stop losses – set them at a decent point away from your trade. That's because, during the first few minutes of trading spreads can be stupidly wide and you could get caught out and stopped out on one rogue early trade. I've had horror stories from several readers of getting stopped out early in the morning by some rogue trade. And if your spread firm is especially nasty they might even close you out on purpose!

My use of stop losses

How do I use stop losses? Well, perhaps I am slightly unconventional!

I only use them on 'buy' trades and not on shorts. Mainly because in my experience when you're in an up trade, a profit warning, or a political event beyond my control could see my share dive overnight. In which case, I think a guaranteed stop loss is pretty much essential. It means if some awful unexpected event occurred, at least my losses would be limited.

However, I don't use stop losses at all on shorts.

Why's that, you undisciplined trader you?

Well, I find it's unusual for a share to jump higher overnight. There's hardly ever a big political event that would shift a share so much higher that quickly. Even the capture of Saddam Hussein did not suddenly put a rocket up shares! Very good news or results can lift shares but they only tend to go up gradually.

So, that's my reasoning. Hope it makes sense. It does to me.

But you must handle and control your stop losses in the best way you can and learn by experience. It could well be that the best plan is to use guaranteed stop losses on all your trades. At least then you know, and can control, your maximum possible loss.

Dangers of over exposure

When you're spread betting you get exposure to shares without putting up all the money you'd have to betting on a normal account. That's kind of good and bad news. Basically the spread firms will let you trade on what's called 'margin'. So you can buy or short a share without putting up the money.

For example, I could buy £10 a point of BSkyB giving me, in effect, exposure to £5,000 of shares without having to put up the five grand. Most spread firms will allow you to trade that with only 10% upfront – so you'd only need to have £500 in your account.

Note

This is where you have to be careful and make sure you are not playing with money you can't afford to lose.

What happens if the shares sink 200 points and you suddenly owe £2,000. Can you afford to pay? And what happens if you open a lot of trades and they all go wrong, leaving you with a whopping great bill?

Always check your spread account. Think about a few worst case scenarios and check carefully you are not overdoing it buying or shorting shares 'on tick'.

Margin calls

This is a call you don't want to get! I'm glad to say I haven't had one since 1999!

A 'margin call' means one, or some, of your positions are losing heavily and the spread firm wants to see the colour of your money. Don't worry, they are very discreet, so if you don't want your missus to know you've been losing she won't find out. They will normally ask you for the money needed to cover some of the losses you are racking up. The best solution is to use a debit card and hand the money over right away.

Is it a wake up call?

If you get a margin call you may also want to consider whether it is a 'wake up call'. Have your positions got away from you and should you close out, take the loss and 'go flat' for a few days? Are you definitely playing with money you can afford to lose?

Be honest with yourself. Don't pretend the losses aren't too bad and you're 'gonna get them back'.

When you get the margin call, give yourself that wake up call!

How I use spread betting

My main uses of spread betting are (in no particular order):

- Shorting FTSE 100 and FTSE 250 companies.
- Buying companies when I'm out of cash in my ISA.
- Buying or selling the FTSE 100 Index.

I treat most trades as short-term (anything between a week and three months).

Note

The major lesson I've learned with spread betting is: keep an open mind and change strategies as the market changes.

For example, don't think: "I think the market's going up all this year so I'm just going to long stocks." Or just short and nothing else. I find a thoughtful mix of long and shorts pays off.

Opening an account

There used to be only two companies that took spread bets – IG Index and City Index, but now there are a host of different spread bet companies, with various different offerings.

I have used a number of these companies and I think it's unfair of me to start slagging off individual ones. That's mainly because I'm a great big coward and I don't want to be the subject of legal action! Also, companies change and it would be unfortunate if I criticised a company here and by the time this book was published that company had changed for the better.

Many traders have two or three accounts open and use different firms depending on a particular trade. Some firms specialise in tiny bets, others have minimum stakes. Some have smaller spreads than others.

Note Beware of firms that offer very small spreads. Remember, they have to make a profit somewhere. You may find (and there are instances of this I know of) trouble 'closing out' a trade. The spread may mysteriously move against you when you try and take your profit or loss.

Some companies take what can be described as an adversarial stance against you. You put on trades and they don't take out a similar trade in the market to ride the trade with you and just make money on the extra spread. In effect, they want you to lose! They want your trade to go wrong and so they cash in. In particular they will do this against clients who mainly lose.

Personally, I use Cantor Index for nearly all my trades now. That's simply because I know for a fact that nearly all trades are hedged in the market so they don't care whether you win or lose. In fact, Cantor would rather you won. A winning client is more likely to carry on spread betting, and so make them a profit, than one who is losing. He or she is more likely to call it a day after racking up losses. They are also fun to deal with and answer the phone quickly.

It's up to you to pick one or two firms – get to know them and see if you like the way you get treated. If you don't like them, there will always be plenty of others!

One way of choosing could be to scan through the bulletin boards and read about the experiences of others. There's a good bulletin board at ADVFN entitled 'spread betting'. Investors there discuss the ins and outs of spread betting and criticise or praise companies.

Credit accounts

Generally most City spread betting is done using credit accounts. When you open your account you can set your credit limit. As spread betting is tightly regulated, the spread firm will want to see you have ready assets to sell should it have to ask you for money. So if you want a credit limit of £5,000 you will have to show you have three times that in ready funds. Cash, shares you own, premium bonds, savings accounts can all be taken into account. Once a year they will usually ask you again for proof of funds. It's not that they don't trust you, but they are forced to do it by the regulators.

Secrets of the winners

At a dinner recently I met a top market maker from a spread betting company. Luckily he was on the pissed side so I thought I'd ask him while he was in that state what makes a spread betting winner...and loser!

I asked: "So what are the trading patterns of the people who win...and what about the people that lose?" His answer was rather revealing.

He said:

"The people that win don't trade as much as the people that lose!"

I've already talked about over-trading earlier in the book. But this seems to be the key to not losing your shirt.

The next secret he let me into was:

"Winners are often those who ask for spreads on firms I've never heard of, rather than the FTSE 100 companies."

Hmm. Interesting! Looks like those who've done their research on some of the smaller companies end up in the money.

And another secret:

"Winners often go flat."

He doesn't mean winners go on a diet, he means they simply close down all their trades, take profits and losses and simply have a few days without a trade on their account at all.

"It seems to refresh their brains, and clear things out."

He also explained sometimes a big winner can turn into an equally big loser:

"I've seen winning accounts turn into losing accounts because the trader gets overconfident and starts playing with much bigger stakes."

What about shorters and buyers, I wondered. Which trades make the money?

> *"Shorters have definitely made more money since 2001," "Of course that's because the markets have mainly been going down. But since the market uptrend started in 2004, those who long are getting the upper hand."*

He also revealed those who hung onto trades for too long tended to lose out:

> *"Spread betting is a short-term tool, those holding onto positions for too long often make a loss."*

So maybe that'll help you before you go plunging into too many trades. I just hope the chap I spoke to doesn't come after me for a fee for using his quotes in the book. Pass the wine, there's a good chap!

Naked Trader's Ten Golden Rules For Spread Betting

1. Think of it for short-term trading only.

2. Clear your account and go flat sometimes.

3. Don't open too many positions.

4. Keep stakes to a level you can afford.

5. Be strict with your stop losses.

6. Make sure you know what you're doing!

7. Remember to trade the opposite way when closing.

8. A margin call could be a 'wake up call'

9. Consider a guaranteed stop loss on every trade.

10. Don't tell the wife how much you're losing.

Directory

It's worth a look around the various spread betting firms' websites. Many of them give you an area where you can practise trading.

And why not open up more than one account? I do suggest to make Cantor Index one of them as I really feel I can vouch for the company!

Here's a list of websites:

- www.cantorindex.co.uk

- www.capitalspreads.com

- www.cityindex.co.uk

- www.cmcmarkets.co.uk

- www.finspreads.com

- www.igindex.co.uk

- www.spreadex.com

- www.tradindex.com

Recommended reading

If my explanations have given you a headache and you still can't get your head around spread betting try the beginner's book:

The Beginner's Guide to Financial Spread Betting by Michelle Baltazar.

On the other hand if you're feeling quite cocky and understand everything easily, try the more advanced:

How to Win at Financial Spread Betting by Charles Vintcent.

Available from the bookshop on my website: www.nakedtrader.co.uk.

15

Advanced Topics

Shorting – making money when shares fall

One of the major uses of spread betting is shorting, where you are doing the opposite of buying a share - you effectively make money if the stock goes *down*.

I would urge new investors to tread carefully before getting into shorting, but it's something that must be considered because it means you can make money during a period where the market is going down. And while I urge caution it is something you should learn about quite quickly.

You can also short indices like the FTSE 100 or the Dow.

There are various ways of shorting - using Contracts For Differences (CFDs), covered warrants and spread betting. But the easiest method is to spread bet. That would certainly be the method I would use first.

I usually have at least two short positions open.

Markets often turn down for quite a while and shorting could be the only way to make money. I tend to only take out short positions in quite large companies. The reason is mainly the spread. The spread firms usually quote much bigger spreads in smaller companies and for shorting purposes I find the spread is simply too much.

Obviously, the best years to take out short positions were in 2000 and 2001 because the market was tumbling and tech shares were being hammered. During those years I held more shorts than 'longs' (buys) because it made sense. I believe at some point in the future I will do the same again.

But I do look on shorting as generally a short-term activity - anything from two weeks to six months.

Hedging

Many investors use shorting as what's called a 'hedge'. No, that's not something that separates you from the nosy neighbours, it's a way of protecting a long position. For example, you may hold 5,000 shares in a company, but are worried for a short-term period (perhaps the company is about to announce results). You could sell the shares, and buy them back after the cloud has passed; but that could be very expensive (what with broker's commission and stamp duty). An alternative is to hold the shares, but take out a down spread bet in the company to an equivalent value of your holding. If bad things do happen, and the share price falls, the amount you lose on your share holding will be approximately offset by the gains in your spread bet trade.

Finding shorts

So how do you go about finding shares that are going to go down and make you money?

Well, strangely enough, you have to do the exact opposite of finding buys. You need to look for shares that are overvalued, on a downtrend, or if the market is in a downturn a share that should sink with it.

I am personally not much cop at trading indices, but I can see the point of holding a FTSE short if you're generally holding loads of share buys. Because if something happens, like a terrorist event, and the FTSE 100 goes into freefall and your shares with it, at least you'll make some money. However, I would advise you to hold off from shorting indices until you are confident in your trading.

Here are the kinds of things I look for in shares I'd like to be short of:

- **Profit warning**
  These tend to come in threes. If a share issues a profit warning there could be worse to come. This could be a good time to short. For example, Courts began issuing profit warnings long before they went bust – you could have shorted and made a killing.

- **General downtrend**
  A share that just keeps going down, maybe breaking through 52 week lows. It often means there is something amiss.

- **High PE**
  If a company has a very high PE or it's making, say, £5 million but has a market cap of £280 million it may be all the promise shown by the company is already in the price and it could fall heavily on any negative news.

- **Watch for 'challenging'!**
  Check the latest reports on the share you're interested in shorting. If you see the words 'challenging', 'difficulties' or 'problems' – could be worth a go!

Some short DON'TS

- Don't go against the trend and short a share because it's already gone up a lot. It could go up a hell of a lot more!

- Don't short a share because some big market guru has. He's probably already in at a better price and he might be wrong.

- Don't short shares in a strong, generally rising market. Even if you're right and it's a bad share, it could still go up with the market.

CFDs

These are a more and more popular way of trading and it's not surprising. You don't have to pay stamp duty, commissions are low and the bid-offer spread is usually very thin. CFDs are probably now the instrument of choice for very active, short-term traders.

> **Note**
>
>
>
> I would advise new investors to avoid them to begin with as it's too easy to trade these using credit and they could lead you to overtrade.

I don't tend to use them for the moment because profits are subject to capital gains tax unlike spread betting. However I am looking at using CFD's to short shares in my self-invested pension plan (SIPP).

If CFDs interest you, make sure you read up as much as you can about them and only go ahead when you're sure you know everything.

As this is generally a book for beginners I'm going to leave it there – but generally look on CFDs as for short-term trading.

Covered warrants

I made a speech at some conference a while back and on after me was a speaker dealing with covered warrants. After he'd spoken for ten minutes my wife nudged me and whispered: "Look at that row over there, they're all fast asleep."

And indeed they were.

I think it's just that 'covered warrants' sound extremely boring, and they're also quite difficult to explain.

Which is quite handy for me, as this book is for beginners and they are a complex derivative, so I'm not going to cover them in depth here.

Rather handy, as it would take me a lot of time and effort to explain them properly!

If you want to learn about them, go to my website (www.nakedtrader.co.uk) and press the bookstore button. Order the book *Covered Warrants* by Andrew Mchattie. He is the expert on covered warrants and the book will tell you everything you need to know.

Warrants *are* useful and I expect to use them if I need to do any shorting for my pension fund. However, for the moment...

> **Note**
>
> If you are a real beginner, I would suggest you leave covered warrants alone until you've had at least one year's experience of the markets.

SIPPS

Or the snappy: 'self-invested personal pension'. It means you can take control of your own pension fund rather than letting the 'professionals' look after your fund.

I'm not going to go into SIPPs in great depth because generally this book is for beginners, and if you are a real beginner, you need to find your feet in the markets before taking the plunge. The question is:

Should you take the plunge and run the fund yourself?

The answer is: could you do any worse than the fund managers?

I watched the pension fund I had with the company I worked for go up for a few years and then sink like a stone between 1999 and 2001, at which point I'd had enough. So when I left full-time work I immediately transferred all the money from two frozen company pensions into my SIPP and began trading.

I'm glad I did as I nearly doubled my money in three years.

So I run my own pension fund, buying and selling shares. Now, of course, I'm confident when it comes to dealing in shares. You need to think carefully about whether to try and run your own fund.

For this section, I'm going to assume you feel reasonably confident. So I'm going to discuss how to set up a SIPP and what to do with the money once you get hold of it.

Setting up a SIPP

Setting up a SIPP, how can I put this? Well, it's a pain in the bum to be frank, especially when you want to transfer in frozen or current pension schemes. It takes ages and there are lots of forms to complete. It also takes a lot of hassling. The reason is of course the people currently running your fund don't want you to quit and run your own. They want to continue receiving their nice fat juicy fees.

Say you want to go for it and start running your own pension fund – what on earth do you do?

Assuming you mainly want to trade shares you need two things:

1. an execution-only **stock broker**; and

2. a **pension trustee**.

The trustee basically looks after the money and keeps it secure for you - usually for a yearly fee of around £150-£300. You then trade the shares as normal and hopefully watch your fund rise.

It's probably best to choose the broker first - maybe the one you use for normal dealings - they should have a list of trustees they recommend and work with. Trustees are much of a muchness. Just choose the cheapest.

It's slightly easier if you want to start from scratch, without transferring in any money.

From April 2006 you can transfer in as much of your salary as you want – you then get 20% added or 40% depending on your tax bracket.

You just send the money to the trustee, it's put into your stock broking account and away you go – buy and sell shares using the money as you wish – and that includes AIM shares which aren't allowed in an ISA.

Transferring frozen schemes

You can transfer in frozen schemes. You have to chase up the company the schemes are lodged with as they need to send you forms (yawn!). You fill them out and send them back the forms – they should then release the money to your trustee.

It can take weeks and you need to keep hassling all the time. Two other bits of hassle to tell you about are:

1. Firstly it can be difficult to transfer in a **final salary scheme**. Some trustees won't let you do it because final salary schemes are supposed to be the bees knees.

2. Secondly there is something called '**protected rights**' – this will be a small part of your frozen pension that, er, is protected for you. Don't ask me why, except it's extremely stupid. You can't put protected rights into a SIPP. You have to leave this money with a building society, bank or fund.

Anyway, all the hassle is worth it in the end. It's a great feeling to be in charge of your own destiny.

You can carry on trading your SIPP till you're 75, at which point the Government reckons you'll be too ga ga to trade any more, and you can take half the balance in cash and buy an annuity with the rest.

Trading in a SIPP

Once you have your SIPP what sort of shares should you deal in?

You really ought to be sensible. You probably have many years to go before you want to cash it in. Don't go crazy – buy some decent, sensible shares with good yields. You're looking for a decent lift for the fund over time.

Look for shares you'd be happy to hold for a while and follow the practices I've already outlined in this book.

Aim for growth of around 10% a year – the fund will soon grow nicely at this rate. Don't take too many risks as you may be relying on this money in the future.

As well as buying shares within a SIPP, you can short too. This can be done by buying covered warrants or CFDs. You'll need to research these carefully.

This book is about shares but I should mention, that from 2006 you can buy residential property within a SIPP and even wine and lots of other investments apart from shares.

I only buy shares within my SIPP as that's what I'm good at!

SIPPS summary

- You can run your own pension fund.
- You can make contributions and transfer in frozen pensions.
- You need a stock broker and a pension trustee.
- It can take time to transfer in funds.
- Buy any shares you like including AIM.
- Be cautious with your fund – you may need the money.

16

Market Miscellany

*Yes, you guessed it, these are the bits
and pieces that don't go anywhere else!*

Rights issues/open offers

Occasionally, a letter from your broker will land on your doormat telling you a company you have shares in is having a rights issue or open offer. This means the company wants to raise more money and is basically asking shareholders to stump up more cash. You then have to decide whether to buy more shares in the company.

The decision is generally quite an easy one.

The shares will be offered to you at a lower price than the current market price. So, say the shares are 120p in the market, the new shares may be offered at something like 100p. You normally have around four weeks to decide whether or not to take up the shares.

The main thing you have to ask yourself is:

> "Do you think the company is going places and are the new shares at a good discount?"

It is easy to miss announcements for these offers, but stock brokers will try and contact investors to advise them what is happening. For example, an open offer came in recently from a company in my portfolio, Sondex, an oil equipment producer. The offer was one new share for every three shares I hold at 160p. As the shares were 190p in the market I was more than happy to buy new shares at 160p! It would mean an instant profit for me if the shares remain above 160p.

Companies normally ask for extra money because they want to grow the business further and this can be good news for long-term investors. Of course it does also mean there are more shares on the market. Sometimes companies launch 'rescue' offers because they could go out of business and need more money to survive.

I usually take new shares, if they are nicely above the offer price, close to the acceptance deadline. Then I look carefully at the company's record and consider whether the shares are likely to blossom.

Sondex wanted to raise money to fund the acquisition of Geolink, which, like Sondex, supplies the oil industry with equipment. The acquisition looks sensible to me!

Investment trusts

These are often overlooked by investors but I've bought a few of these and made some decent profits.

What investment trusts do is buy shares in other companies. They can be bought just like normal shares – there's a buying and a selling price. Usually the investment trust has a 'theme', so it will buy shares of a particular kind and, in some cases, buy shares in other investment trusts.

For example, one investment trust I have profited from in the past is Resources Investment Trust [RIT], who buys shares in gold and mining companies. The argument being that if you buy RIT, you're getting exposure to this sector, diversified across a number of shares, and the benefits of a fund manager who knows the sector and does the legwork of research for you to select the best companies. Okay, it doesn't always work out like that, but that's the theory.

Alternatively, if you fancy getting exposure to the Japanese market you could buy a Japanese investment trust (IT). There are many types of ITs specialising in smaller companies, pharmaceuticals, German markets etc. The list is endless.

Are they worth buying?

Well, why not? Personally, I don't buy that many or that often and I treat buying them like any other share. You have to research investment trusts in a completely different way to buying a share.

First, and most important, is to discover what's called the 'net asset value' (NAV) of an investment trust. This is a rough calculation of the value of the fund at a point in time.

Resources Investment Trust

Let's look at Resources Investment Trust (RIT).

The code is REI so off to ADVFN to take a look. Get to the 'Quote page'. You can see under the news section, RIT publishes its NAV once a day. This is a bit unusual – most ITs publish NAVs once a week. The other way to find the NAV is click on 'financials' and you'll see the NAV quoted there.

So the NAV for RIT on July 19th was 120p. And the share price was 95p.

It may seem odd to you that the share price is way below the NAV, but it's fairly standard – most investment trust share values are at a discount to the NAV. The amount of discount depends on how risky the market thinks the shares or assets held by the trusts are.

In RITs case the discount is around 25%. This is quite high, so RIT is in the risky category.

The next step is to discover some of the shares or assets held by RIT. Easy enough. Dip into the news stories list on ADVFN and there it is under 'top ten holdings'. I click on that and, lo and behold, a list of their major holdings. It's now a question of looking at the holdings and deciding whether you want exposure to some of those stocks.

For example, their biggest holding is in Emerald Energy, a small oil exploration company. I can see Emerald is a tiny penny share trading at one and a half pence. Immediately you can see how risky that holding is. In fact, the top ten holdings are pretty much all risky companies. However, because the trust holds a large number of shares, the value of the trust might only slump a small amount if Emerald went bust. Of course the upside could be great. I can see from the various NAVs that the net asset values are very volatile.

In summary, if I bought RIT I would be buying a high risk trust. Which might be a solid move to pep up a low risk portfolio.

For example, your portfolio could be full of safe-ish, slow-moving stocks and RIT might give it a bit of life. And if you think risky mining and gold stocks could rise, the trust will give you a good spread of exposure, rather than you having to go in and buy just one of these risky shares.

It worked for me! I bought RIT at 76p and sold at 105p to make a decent profit.

Looking at other trusts – how else could you easily get exposure to, say, emerging markets? Maybe you want a bit of exposure to booming markets in other countries. So you could try something like the Baring Emerging Markets IT.

Certainly having one or two ITs in a portfolio could be a solid move. But if you choose a risky one it will certainly be worth imposing a fairly tight stop loss.

Investments trusts' summary

- Research like normal shares.
- Check the net asset value.
- Find out the top holdings.
- Work out how risky/volatile the trust is.
- Make sure you want exposure to its particular market.

Share buybacks

Sometimes you'll see a company announce that it is going to 'buyback' some of its shares. Companies can seek authorisation from its shareholders to do this. Generally, companies seek to buyback their shares because they feel the market is undervaluing their shares and the price is too low. By starting a buyback programme, the value of the shares are usually underpinned by the buybacks and the shares might gradually see a rise in value.

But I'm not a great fan of buybacks. If the market is undervaluing the company then there is probably a good reason. So don't rely on buybacks to improve the value of the share you are holding by that much.

I would even consider selling the shares concerned, because buybacks, in my experience, don't tend to lead to fireworks for the share price.

However, for those wanting a steady income from a steady share, I suppose a buyback programme would give you confidence that the share will have some support.

Shareholders' meetings

If you're a shareholder of any company you're entitled to go along to the Annual General Meeting (AGM). These are usually pretty dull affairs, but if you've got a long-term holding in the company it maybe worth considering.

Sometimes, companies even invite shareholders round to have a look.

Visiting Vanco

One day I was invited as a shareholder to an afternoon at Vanco, and I decided to go along.

Why not? The shares had done very well. So, why not find out more about a company I've invested in? Anyhow, I spent three very interesting hours there.

It was quite amusing when I arrived. I was expecting hordes of eager shareholders ready to find out all about the company they'd invested money in. But the girl at reception looked at me blankly when I mentioned the meeting. Then she remembered, "Oh yes, please sit over there". I was joining the only other two shareholders who had turned up. I think they were as embarrassed as me and we all pretended to read the thoughtfully provided newspapers.

After a while we were invited to the boardroom and we were outnumbered by the good bosses of Vanco. One of the shareholders turned out to have a son working there and the other one simply went to all the meetings he was invited to. There was even free tea and biscuits! (Jammy dodgers, very nice.)

Joking aside, I'm glad I went because I really enjoyed it.

I discovered a company that is very dynamic, very focussed and knows exactly what it's doing, where it's going and how it's going to get there. The most telling thing for me, and it might only be a small detail but I think it's very important, was the company's obvious dedication to its customers.

John Locke, the very impressive and irrepressible chief technical officer, showed us round the technical areas. As he showed us the area where phone calls from customers come in and their problems are fixed, he told us about their 'ratings system'. When a call to a customer has ended, that customer gets the chance to leave a one to ten rating for how he or she felt the call was handled by Vanco. Any customer that leaves a five or below rating gets a callback within fifteen minutes from one of the company's bosses. That is the kind of attention to detail and service that impresses me.

Elsewhere, workers are incentivised in many ways, and they seemed to really enjoy working there. The shareholder whose son worked there said his son rarely comes home till 10pm because he enjoys the work so much.

At the end of the interesting afternoon, I realised this was a good company that was well managed and I was going to hang onto my shares. I discovered the edge it had over rivals and all questions were well answered.

The visit certainly made me feel like accepting other invites as a shareholder, time permitting.

Note

If an invite lands on your doorstep, don't just bin it – consider going, you never know what you might find out!

I bought Vanco at 185p and eventually sold at 273p to take good profits. I've since re-bought and the shares are soaring. That afternoon out was worth my time...

Share perks

You'll often see articles in newspapers and magazines written by lazy hacks regarding share 'perks'. When I say 'lazy', this is one of the easiest features for them to write as they can re-write a perks feature written previously in about ten minutes!

Perks are 'special' discounts you can get if you buy a certain number of a company's shares. For example, hotel chains might give you 10% off rooms or a holiday company 10% off holidays.

Note

Don't buy shares just because of perks!

You should buy shares to sell them at a profit, whereas all perks do is make you hang onto a share longer than you should. Also, many of these companies only offer perks to those with share certificates rather than through a nominee account.

And you will probably find you could get similar discounts by phoning the company and asking them, shares or no shares!

So forget about perks.

Websites worth a look!

There are tons of financial websites out there, and most of them, today, are actually very good. That's generally because the people that set them up enjoy finance and shares and that tends to come across. The people that write for them are also very keen and enjoy what they do.

Most of them provide a decent amount of free information, then you pay a bit extra for 'premium' information – that usually means: always-on access to real-time share prices; certain research tools and the like. For example, once you've had some experience you may want to access level 2 services, which will cost something like £40-50 a month.

The sites tend to offer premium material all priced around the same level, but you may want to shop around. Best thing is to experiment, but you'll probably end up using two or three sites.

For brand new starters you probably only need the free stuff to begin with. As you get more experienced you may need to start paying for decent access to real-time information.

ADVFN

www.advfn.com

This is the number one site. I've mentioned it a lot in this book, and I use it all the time. Live prices and great research tools. Just use the free stuff to begin with. I've negotiated a deal with ADVFN so you can get access to their premium lists and bulletin board – it's £40 a year instead of £60. (Or only £3.33 a month!) This means you get access to my 'naked trader discussion forum', where you can chat to me and some very decent traders online. Just call 0870 794 0236 and ask for the 'Naked Trader Bronze membership offer'.

Naked Trader

www.nakedtrader.co.uk

Er, my website. Bloody good if you ask me.

Hemscott

www.hemscott.com

Worth a look. Plenty of good research material here and a bulletin board worth dipping into from time to time.

The Motley Fool

www.fool.co.uk

Despite its title, quite a serious site. Think pipe and slippers. Some interesting articles though, so may be worth a gander.

MoneyAM

www.moneyam.com

A similar site to ADVFN. It also contains real-time prices, but its bulletin boards don't have as many contributors. Handy as an alternative to ADVFN and I use it as a back-up should ADVFN go down.

Citywire

www.citywire.co.uk

Breaking City news. I don't use it much, but I know a lot of investors do.

The Welsh Wizard

www.thewelshwizard.com

A website written by a real trader and jolly good he is too. Interesting articles written by a genuinely interesting market maverick. Read all about the music of share charts!

ShareCrazy

www.sharecrazy.com

Interesting site that seems aimed at those very new to the market.

Books

Read. And read some more. I know this book is superb but you should be reading others too.

There are loads of books out there and I've read a whole load of them. I've never regretted buying a single one because, generally, there's always a gem or two of decent information and points to think about.

So here are a few I very strongly recommend. They are in no particular order. They are all excellent reads for stock market beginners and old hands alike.

The Disciplined Trader by Mark Douglas

An excellent look at good trading practices, including a look at why what's in your mind can affect your trading. There are also some tips on how to become a profit-making trader.

Online Investing by Stephen Eckett

Stephen knows everything there is to know about investing from many years of experience. All the questions you ever wanted to know about online investing are answered here – written clearly and easily. It's a must-have reference work. (Do you think I've been nice enough about his book as he's edited this one?)

The Schwartz Stock Market Handbook by David Schwartz

David Schwartz uses historical trends to try and outfox the market. I've met David and he certainly persuaded me that following historical trends can be profitable. Which days are the best days to trade and the worst? Why is it worth buying the Footsie just before Christmas? Decide for yourself whether you should look at history before trading.

High Probability Trading by Marcel Link

This book tries to teach all those who want to trade the mindset of a successful trader. What you should think before you reach for the buy button. No complex material, just good common sense.

Investor's Guide to Selecting Shares that Perform by Richard Koch

This book uncovers ten ways to beat the market, and there are some very good ideas here. A good broad discussion of methods you can use to try and outperform the indices. I learned a number of excellent tips and I agree with pretty much everything Richard says.

Come Into My Trading Room by Dr Alexander Elder

This one must be the book I've read and re-read the most. Entering Dr Elder's trading room is a very interesting experience. His years of profitable trading show through the pages and many of his warnings regarding some of the pitfalls of trading are excellent. I think this one is an especially good read if you have never traded before. There is also plenty of market psychology discussed, one of my favourite topics. And talking of psychology...

Investment Madness by John R Nofsinger

Subtitled: 'How psychology affects your investing and what to do about it.' This is one of the must reads! It is highly amusing but also very sharp. You may recognise your own character traits in the book – and once you recognise them, you can learn how to stop your own character from ruining your trades. Topics include the problems of overconfidence, social aspects of investing, the 'double or nothing mentality' and seeking pride and avoiding regret.

The Investor's Guide to Charting by Alistair Blair

'Analysis for the intelligent investor.' (So if you're a bit thick better read something else!) But seriously, for those of you who decide charting is the way to work out which shares to sell and buy, this is the easiest read. Alistair explains the art of a chart and what it's all about. Find out what all the chart jargon means like 'double tops' and whether charting is suitable for you. And what's really good is he discusses how much of chart theory and practice should be taken with a pinch of salt.

Technical Analysis Plain And Simple by Michael Khan

This one is worth buying in conjunction with the Blair book above. As the title suggests, a good plain guide to the world of TA and charting.

Technical Analysis For Dummies by Barbara Rockefeller

The title sums it up I guess! More on charting for beginners here. She certainly treats the reader like a dummy, but that's no bad thing when it comes to learning all about TA.

The Beginner's Guide To Financial Spread Betting by Michelle Baltazar

I hope I've given you some idea what spread betting is all about in this book. This is a comprehensive guide for beginners, so if you don't know your shorts from your margins, this is the one for you. If you already spread bet and know what you're doing, then this is not a buy. For beginners only. But if you already spread bet and want some strategies then the following book is the one for you...

How To Win At Financial Spread Betting by Charles Vintcent

This one covers all kinds of different strategies for making real profits by spread betting. Charles patiently explains how he does it – and the good news is he is a real trader! Some thought-provoking material for those of you who are already happily trading.

The Investors Guide To Understanding Accounts by Robert Leach

This may sound like a really boring one but actually Robert has turned what could be a very unexciting subject into an interesting one. Ever wondered how to look at a set of accounts and know whether it's all good or there is trouble ahead? Are they cooking the books? There's also an excellent ten point summary which will point you in the right direction.

The eBay Book by David Belbin

A bit off topic but a great guide on how to sell and buy things on eBay. Could this book turn you into an eBay millionaire?

You can order any of these through my website, www.nakedtrader.co.uk. Delivery is usually very fast and often next day.

I keep my website updated with reviews of the latest books as they are published, so do check in for those.

17

And Finally…

The Naked Trader Rules

I'm not really one for rules. I've always hated authority, so rules and me don't often get along. But I thought to finish up I'd set out a few investing rules especially for the new investor.

You're not going to lose everything you have if you don't follow them. But after you finish reading this book and it's tossed on top of a lot of other dusty financial tomes...and you come back to it one day...these rules are a pretty good summary of what I've been banging on about.

They are in no particular order. In other words number 1 has no more importance to it than number 30. This is not the chart show.

The Rules

1. Only play with money you can really afford to lose. Be honest with yourself.
2. Understand as fully as you can everything about a company before you buy it.
3. Don't rush into anything or chase a share price. There's always another share coming along in a minute.
4. Don't buy shares the day after a tip. The prices will have risen already (even before the market opens) and you'll be paying too much for them.
5. Be wary of buying into systems promising you thousands for no work. If it's too good to be true it probably is.
6. Don't buy a share because someone on a bulletin board says it's going to double.
7. Resist the immediate urge to buy a penny share because it could make you money quickly.
8. Cut your losses fast if you bought a share and it's tanking.
9. Don't take profits too quickly. If you've got a good share and it's slowly heading up, stick with it.
10. Don't be panicked out of a good share if it goes down for a day. The market makers may be trying to get your shares cheaply.
11. Beware of buying a share just because a director bought some. They often get it wrong.
12. If you are buying more than £3,000 of a small share, check its normal market size. If that is below £1,000 of shares you may have trouble when it comes to selling them.
13. Never catch a falling knife. That means don't buy a share because it's gone down a lot. Better to buy shares that are going up. That bargain may end up even cheaper.
14. Read! Buy investment books and then buy some more. You can never learn too much.
15. Don't buy a share after a profit warning (they often come in threes).

16. Check the spread between the buying and selling prices. If it's more than 5%, the share could be far too risky.

17. Beware of buying before 9am – the spreads can be at their widest. Don't be suckered into buying a share at a silly price early on.

18. Don't buy and sell indices like the FTSE 100 or the Dow, especially if you are a new investor. This is just gambling.

19. Be careful of mining and oil exploration stocks. One bad report can see these shares tumble and they are impossible to value properly.

20. Don't buy companies that are making a loss. You're gambling they'll make a profit one day. It may never happen.

21. Don't buy a share because it has a perk like discounted hotel rooms.

22. Spread betting should only be considered only for short-term trades.

23. Use stop losses. Set them around 10% away from your buying price and don't hesitate to act on them.

24. Try and have a plan with every share. Think about what your exit price will be.

25. Shares are for buying AND selling. Do run profits but also take them sometimes.

26. Don't get involved with things you don't understand. So don't buy CFDs or covered warrants if you don't fully understand them.

27. Beware of trading too much on margin. Think about what your losses could be and whether you can afford to cover them.

28. If you're losing heavily it may be best to cut all your positions and come back to the market another time.

29. Don't over-trade. Keep to about 8-10 open positions. Any more and you are going to have trouble keeping on top of them.

30. Beware of overconfidence. If you're on a winning run don't start increasing the size of your positions.

31. Don't only go long, do think about shorting stocks, but this is not for beginners.

32. Be careful about relying on one method of stock picking. Cover all the angles.

33. Never buy a share without doing any research.

34. Try and specialise in a small number of stocks – follow 20 or 30, not 100.

35. Always check your ex-dividend dates. Your share will fall on this date for the amount of the dividend, so don't panic.

36. Open more than one broking account. Then you can compare their services and systems.

37. Don't trade too much 'on margin'. You may take on too many positions that you can't afford.

38. Read the financial press – some of it is rubbish but you must keep in touch with what's going on.

39. Take a complete break from trading sometimes. We all need a holiday.

40. Remember the good advice of Corporal Jones in Dad's Army: "Don't panic!"

Some Final Naked Thoughts

That's it!

I've pretty much finished. And believe me, as I sit here writing these words I am feeling very happy. Writing this book has taken me back to my school days as it's been like having homework every night.

I now have great admiration for anyone that's written a book. It really is hard work. And don't think I'm making my millions out of this – not at £1.66 a sale I'm not! (NB Thanks for the £1.66 – that's three tubs of premium cat food and she's very grateful.)

I've just come off the phone, I've negotiated a better deal – £1.67. I'm pretty cute, huh?

The real reason I ended up writing this was a desire to stop new investors making the same stupid mistakes I made when I started. I hope the tenner or so you paid for this will seem like a very small amount for what I hope I will save you by...saving you from yourself.

I'm pretty certain 80% of new investors will follow the same tried and trusted path of getting it completely and utterly wrong, in the first year at least.

What's the most important lesson I can end with?

I think it must be avoid temptation and greed. What I mean by that is avoid temptation to buy shares that obviously carry a big risk to your capital. I know it's exciting to play with fire, but I promise you that you'll get burned.

The biggest tip I can give you is to avoid being greedy. Try and aim for a sensible return on your money rather than trying to double it in a week. If you start off putting ten grand in, be sensible and aim to try and make 20% on it, or two grand over a year. If you achieve that, give yourself a cheer, because that's 15% more than you'd get in a building society.

Stick with sensible companies with real profits who pay dividends. Ignore the tiny penny shares or illiquid companies. Try not to follow tipsters or believe you will double your money in a few days. I get emails every day from tipping companies advising buys in the smallest companies with huge spreads that could just as easily go bust as double. Be strong and ignore them. Pick the best companies you can find. Remember it's investing, not gambling.

And please be brave. If you make a mistake and buy a share that starts falling heavily, get out! Admit your losses and mistakes and cut them early before too much damage is done.

And talking of damage, make sure you can really afford to be investing in shares. Look at the money you're putting in and be honest. Can you really afford to lose a lot of it? If you can't, put it in a building society! The market is cut-throat and the weak and undisciplined are soon reeling from losses. Don't let this person be you – I want *you* to be a winner.

Once again, I reiterate: I am nothing special. *You* can be a stock market winner as well. Put in the hours and the practice and don't expect instant riches. Think of the market as a way to get rich...slowly!

Finally, and this might sound odd, but have fun with your investments! Enjoy the up days and celebrate your victories. Get the champagne out! Just don't start trading right after drinking it.

Times change quickly with markets and a few things may be out of date if you're reading this, maybe a few years after I wrote it. But that's why I have a website at www.nakedtrader.co.uk. As well as my daily dealings, there's always new material there for you to read and I often discuss the share deals that went wrong and why. You are always welcome to email me through the site. I reply to every mail I get unless it's offering me Viagra (I've already got boxloads of the stuff in the garage).

I wish all readers of this book all the luck in the world with their investing. Get out there and practise a few of the lessons I hope I've taught you.

May your share buys rise, and your share shorts fall (except when there's a lady in the room).

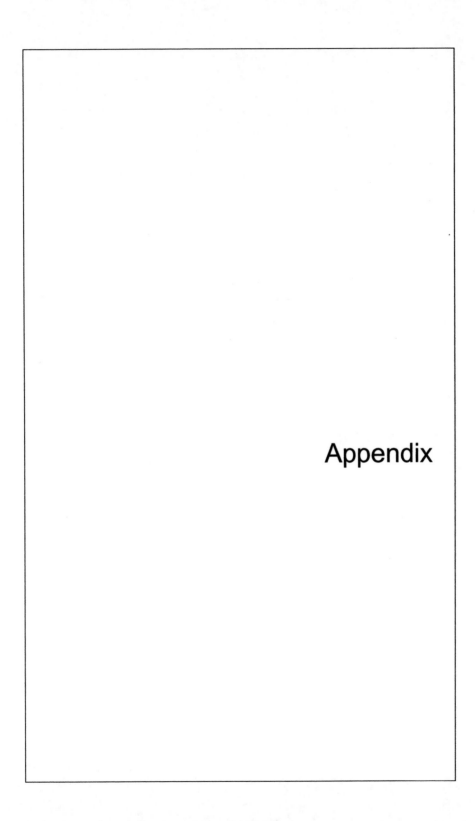

Appendix

On another level – Level 2

This is advanced stuff. I thought it best to put it in the Appendix so it didn't frighten anyone too much!

Firstly, 'level 2' is *not* essential for you to start trading. But perhaps three to six months after starting to trade, it is something you should understand, and I feel all reasonably active investors should consider having a level 2 data service.

It really isn't necessary if you're only buying one share a month, but if you're going to be investing a fair bit I think it's essential. I could not invest without it!

So what the hell is it, why is it worth having?

Let's look at an example. Looking at my ADVFN screen I see that the current price of Diageo shares is 801.5-802 (this is sometimes called the level 1 price). Meaning, that the shares are offered at 802, and being bid at 801.5. But these aren't the only current bids and offers – there might be hundreds of others. The quote that you see on the screen is merely the current *best* bid and offer. So:

- 801.5: is currently the highest bid price.
- 802: is currently the lowest offer price.

There will be many other bids below 801.5. For example, some traders may be bidding at 801, some at 800.5, 800, etc. Likewise, many other traders might be willing to sell Diageo at 802.5, 803, 804, etc. But with a level 1 price, all you see is the best bid and the best offer. You can't see 'below' that, which is a shame, because it would be very useful to know what the other bids in the market are, 'just out of sight'. For example, there could be a huge order lurking to buy millions of Diageo shares at 801. *That* would be useful to know, but you can't tell that with level 1.

You can with level 2.

Level 2 displays all the bids and offers: the volume of shares being bid or offered at every level. It's sometimes described as displaying the depth of the market. It enables the trader to see the profile of all the current orders, and at what levels big orders are likely to be triggered.

For active traders, just having a level 1 service would be like trading blind.

Level 2 basically tells you what's really going on in the market and once you get experienced at using it, short-term you'll be able to predict whether a share is about to go up or down.

The real expert on level 2 is Clem Chambers, who is the boss of ADVFN. Overleaf is an introductory piece by Clem on level 2 for complete beginners.

An introduction to level 2

By Clem Chambers, MD of ADVFN

You may see in the newspaper, or from a site such as ADVFN that a share is 100p. This price is just the tip of the iceberg as there is a lot more information available than the top line figure of a simple share price.

There's the bid and offer representing the price you can buy and sell at, the volume traded so far that day, details of trades that have occurred, the type of trades that made up the trading volume and even values like the average price of the stock over a recent period of trading. In the UK, the London Stock Exchange collects all this information and makes these details available to anyone who is prepared to pay a little for it.

Broadly speaking, there are two levels of price information transmitted by the London Stock Exchange – level 1 and level 2 data.

Level 1 contains the price, bid and offer, volume and trade information. This enables a trader to see trades that have been made, ascertain what type of trade it was and know what the current price of a share is in the market. While level 1 shows the result of trading, level 2 shows the sentiment. It provides greater transparency and actually shows what is going on in the market itself.

In days gone by, the jobber on the floor of the Exchange acted as the wholesaler, the broker acted as an agent/retailer and the investor was the end customer. Investors would instruct their broker, who would then come onto the floor of the Exchange and buy from the jobber. The investor was not allowed to interact with the jobber at all. The jobber held a book, which was his account of the amounts of stock he held. This was his 'order book' and the collective order books of all the jobbers, was the heart of the market.

Today this order book is an electronic one and is contained inside a computer. Level 2 is the status information of this order book.

There are three kinds of level 2 order books: SEAQ, SETS and SETSmm:

1. **SEAQ** is an order book where only market makers can place their bids and offers.
2. **SETS** holds anonymous orders placed by all participants in the market.
3. The new **SETSmm** system, introduced in November 2003 by the London Stock Exchange, is a hybrid allowing both.

Each book is designed as a trading platform for different sizes of listed company. Generally, SETS is for big company stocks with high demand and supply for their shares. SEAQ is for smaller stocks, which trade less actively. SETSmm was introduced for stocks underneath the FTSE 100 in the less active FTSE 250 segment. SEAQ is basically a modern representation of the old jobber system, where stocks and shares would be bought on the floor from a market maker.

SEAQ

On a SEAQ screen a number of market makers put up their buy and sell prices for the shares they make a market in. The market can then see what each particular market maker wants to do on the buy and sell side for each stock. The market maker (modern day jobber) makes his money on the 'spread'.

The spread is the difference between the bid and offer price and represents a margin between what he buys a share at and what he sells at. Just like a wholesaler, he buys low and sells high. In theory he is just a simple facilitator of the market, however there is a lot more to market making than immediately meets the eye.

When you buy a share, your broker will contact a market maker by either calling him up or entering an order on an automated system. In effect the market maker is acting as a one man London Stock Exchange.

However, there are other market makers competing for his bid/offer profit margin. All the market makers are linked together electronically by the Stock Exchange and therefore compete as they once did on the trading floor. SEAQ is the electronic summary of the state of all bids and offers available on a stock made by the market makers. Some shares have a dozen market makers, while some very small companies have only one market maker.

Looking at a SEAQ screen with several market makers on it, you can see that not all of them are what is called 'On the bid' or 'On the offer'. This means they are either quoting to buy a stock at a lower price than other market makers, or will only sell the stock more expensively than other market makers. Being 'Off the bid' or 'Off the offer' means not wanting to trade the share at the current price being offered by other market makers.

When an investor wants to buy a SEAQ stock, his broker calls a market maker buys the stock from him. The details of the transaction will then be registered as a trade with the London Stock Exchange.

It is the state of the bid and offers, put up on the SEAQ level 2 by the market makers, that helps traders and investors discern the state of the market in a SEAQ stock. This is because these positions indicate the appetite of the market for a particular share and hence suggest what might happen next to the price.

SETS

SETS is an automated market maker run by the Stock Exchange. It is the market for the biggest stocks in the UK and is made up of the FTSE 100 constituents and remnants of ex-members of the index.

SETS is an evolution from the old system of market making jobbers and was introduced as the future of the Stock Exchange in the late 90s. The technology facilitated the collection of information generated remotely and enabled it to be centralised at the London Stock Exchange.

SETS stocks are shown on level 2 as an 'order book.' This electronic book has two columns – sell orders and buy orders. These orders are classified as Bids to buy and Offers to sell. Rather than four market makers making four bids and four offers, the order book represents registered offers and bids at a selection of prices, as if there were scores and scores of market makers at many and varied price levels.

Brokers, market makers, traders and private individuals who have a direct connection to the SETS system, place orders in the order book. When someone wants to take up a bid or offer in the book at the stated price, the transaction is executed and it becomes a trade. It is the overall make up of the SETS book that provides the investor with a close up view of the equilibrium of the market. This detailed picture shows what is going on behind the scenes in a share and helps form a further opinion of the balance of supply and demand for a stock. The better the picture you have of the state of the market and the record of the recent history that produced the current price, the easier it is to predict the ensuing outcome.

SETSmm

SETS doesn't show the names of market makers and SEAQ does not allow for all comers to put an order into the market. Including features of both SEAQ and SETS, SETSmm attempts to bridge the gap for medium sized companies.

SETSmm allows an order for stock to enter straight into the market at whatever price and allows a participant to behave just like a market maker. The idea is that this opportunity will stimulate liquidity and competition and bring down the spreads on these smaller stocks. The market maker is still there to guarantee liquidity if the going gets rough, and for that matter make a thin spread, but there is an opportunity for anyone to take on the role of supplier of liquidity in any event. Basically, the order book is made up of anonymous orders like SETS but has named market maker orders too.

Focus on SEAQ

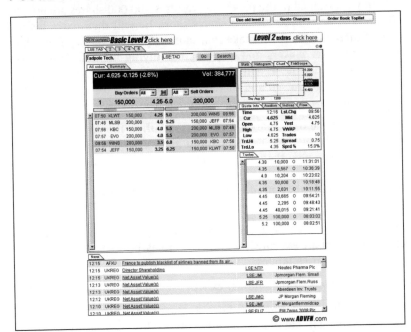

The actual level 2 information is held to the left of the screen. On the left are the Bid prices: the prices at which market makers will buy stock from you. On the right are the prices at which market makers will sell to you. The strip above these quotes contains the highest bid and the lowest offer being put forward by the combined market makers and is the bid/offer spread you see on level 1. The price quoted is normally the 'Mid', the Mid being halfway between the bid/offer.

On the strip on either side of the bid/offer price is a number representing the number of market makers actually at the bid or offer. The balance of market makers is of course information that may lead you to expect a price change.

Market makers still essentially try to sell at the offer and buy at the bid. In an ideal world buyers would match sellers, there would be lots of trades, the price would not move and they would earn the spread in return for facilitating the market. Market makers do not want to hold stock, nor do they want to be short. However, in the real world the balance between buyers and sellers swings to and fro. Market makers therefore have to buy a particular share for an extended period, which they have to hold. Then suddenly, because the shares are in favour, they will have droves of people wanting to buy. Seeing as they do not wish to hold a large inventory of stock, large swings in demand and supply have a dramatic effect of their net position in a stock.

Say a market maker has 100,000 shares in company Bloggs and suddenly it is tipped in the paper. The result is 200,000 shares are bought off him and he is now 100,000 shares short. He will then move his bid up and offer up. This will make him more expensive to buy from than the other market makers and stop anyone buying off him. It will also increase the price he is willing to pay for the stock and hopefully encourage a seller to sell and therefore fill his short position. As the bid and offer has risen, so to has the mid price. The share has gone up.

If he was not the only market maker on the offer, the offer price might not go up, only the Bid. The remaining market makers may have stock to sell. However, now there are less market makers offering at that price, and if buyers continue then the other market makers will have to raise their offer, and if they need to buy new stock they will raise their bid price too.

In the SEAQ book you can see market makers move their bid and offer prices as orders are executed, it is this interplay between market makers that determine price moves.

If there are sellers in the market, exactly the opposite happens.

These are the basic rules of how a market maker's system works. However, like all gaming situations the reality can be a lot more complex.

In a stock with a high level of trade volume and perhaps a low volatility, the spread will be small. This is because the risk to the market maker is low and competition with other market makers attracted to the stock is high.

The movement and size of the spread is also an important indicator for the state of the market in a share and the likelihood of its future movements.

What follows is an example scenario:

There are two market makers in a stock. They are both on the bid and offer, which is 9p and 10p respectively.

Market maker A receives an order at 10p for 100,000 shares. He sells the shares.

He only had 50,000 shares in his book and now has -50,000 shares. He marks his bid/offer to 9.5/10.5. The overall bid/offer is now 9.5/10 so the mid price is 9.75, meaning the price has gone up 0.25.

The next order is a sell of 50,000 shares, which Market maker A buys and therefore closes the short position. His profit on the 100,000 shares is 50,000 x 1p and 50,000 x 0.5p – that is £750.

Meanwhile, another order comes in for 100,000 shares and Market maker B sells them to the customer. Market maker B has 120,000 shares in his book and now only has 20,000. The market is on the rise and he doesn't want to be short in a rising market, so he moves his bid/offer to match Market maker A's bid/offer of 9.5p and 10.5p. The overall bid has not moved but the offer has, so the price goes up another 0.25p.

As you can see the spread 'went in', became smaller as the price rose and 'went out,' got larger again when it rose the second time. ADVFN has a unique tool to watch this process called 'Quote Changes' (see graphic below). It can be accessed from the level 2 screen at the top highlighted.

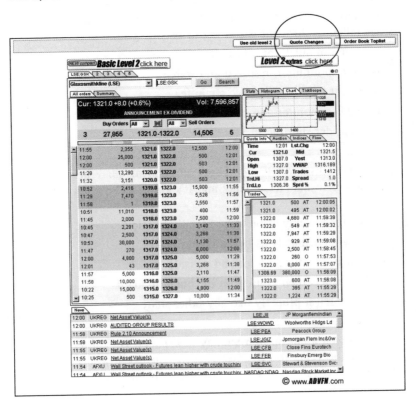

You can see this all unfolding on a level 2 screen. However this is just the start. There are numerous techniques and strategies employed by market participants. The more information and transparency you have, the stronger position you are in.

If you would like to register for 'level 2', ADVFN are offering 15 months for the price of 11 (i.e. 4 months free). Call ADVFN on 0870 7940236 and ask for the 'Naked Trader level 2 offer'.

Quiz – What sort of investor are you?

Here's a fun quiz to test your skills as a potential investor. Answer all the questions honestly. Do not cheat and look over the page for the right answers.

Pick only one answer for each question. Note down the question number and which letter you picked.

Questions

1 You look on ADVFN Toplists and see a share you've never heard of has fallen by 20% but is starting to rise. Do you:

a- Jump in quick for a fast rise

b- Add to monitor, research and watch

c- Grunt then go and have a cup tea

d- Add to monitor and come back to it another day

e- Consider shorting it

2 A friend calls and tells you about an amazing share he's found. It's got a superb new technology and it's going to be a ten bagger. Do you:

a- Pretend to buy some to be friendly but don't

b- Buy immediately as he's a good tipster

c- Put it on your monitor and consider it

d- Buy loads then ramp it on the bulletin boards

e- Research it properly like any other share

3 You've seen a hot tip in a Sunday newspaper. The tipster rates it his buy of the year. You've researched it and like it a lot. The market makers have raised the price substantially before the market opens on Monday. Do you:

a- Buy it the first chance you can

b- Wait for a dip later in the day

c- Buy it a few days later

d- Forget it – the rise is too steep

e- Add to monitor to consider another time

4 You bought a share at 50p and you set a stop loss of 42p. The share has slipped to 40p. Do you:

a- Hold for a bit longer – it'll go up again

b- Sell it immediately

c- Sell half but hold on to the rest

d- Buy more to average down your buying price

e- Check the chart, maybe you set the loss at the wrong price

5 You've spotted a share really close to a 52 week breakout which looks outstanding. Do you:

a- Wait for a bit longer to confirm the breakout

b- Wait and check your research again

c- Buy now before everyone else gets in

d- Check if a statement is due shortly

e- Buy – as there's nothing else you like today

6 You're sitting on a very nice profit of 20% on a share and it exceeded the target price you'd set when you bought it. Do you:

a- Keep holding, and increase the target

b- Keep holding, and shift up stop loss 10%

c- Sell – time to bank a profit

d- Sell half, keep the rest

e- Buy some more, this is a cracker!

7 A company you bought has sunk by 70%. Do you:

a- Say "sod it I can't lose much more" and hold

b- Say "sod it" and sell

c- Say "sod it" and buy more to 'average down'

d- Say "sod it" and pretend you never bought it

e- Say "sod it" and kick the cat

8 You are going to buy a share for the first time ever. You decide to pick it by:

a- Following a tipsheet recommendation

b- Doing careful research

c- Sticking a pin in the *FT* share price lists

d- Going with a hot penny share tipped by someone on a bulletin board

e- Giving Mystic Meg a call

9 Some bloke calls you out of the blue and asks whether you would like to buy shares in an amazing company that's going to rocket. Do you:

a- Put a bit into it, you never know

b- Tell him he must be joking and hang up

c- Ask him whether the FSA would approve of his call

d- Tell him you bought Coffee Republic and have no money left

e- Buy loads. The company sounds reputable and you could make a fortune

10 You've been given £10k as a gift but you can't really afford to lose it. How do you invest the money?

a- Play games of internet poker

b- In the stock market

c- In premium bonds

d- In a high interest account

e- On the 4.45 at Kempton Park

11 You see a picture of The Naked Trader. Do you think:

a- What a handsome man

b- His wife is really lucky

c- What the hell happened to the hair?

d- Isn't that Phil Mitchell from *EastEnders*

e- Wouldn't like to meet him on a dark night

Now look at the key opposite and add up the numbers.

Scores

1-	a-5 b-1 c-2 d-4 e-3
2-	a-1 b-5 c-3 d-5 e-1
3-	a-5 b-4 c-2 d-2 e-1
4-	a-4 b-1 c-2 d-5 e-4
5-	a-2 b-1 c-5 d-2 e-5
6-	a-4 b-1 c-3 d-2 e-5
7-	a-4 b-1 c-5 d-5 e-4
8-	a-5 b-1 c-5 d-5 e-4
9-	a-4 b-1 c-1 d-1 e-5
10-	a-5 b-4 c-1 d-1 e-5

Anyone not answering a or b to question 11 is disqualified from the quiz.

Add up all your scores for your final total.

Analysis

- **15 or below**: Master investor!!!
  You have every chance of success in the stock market. Your approach to shares looks to be solid and I have every confidence that you will soon be in profit.

- **16–25**: Good potential
  You have the makings of a good investor, but you must be careful not to blow it by taking too many risks.

- **26–39**: A lot of work to do
  You are too liable to take major risks and you're likely to make losses unless you temper your gambling instincts.

- **40–50**: You are nuts!
  Stop investing, or should I say gambling, RIGHT NOW and read this book properly all the way through. You are far too gung-ho to be an investor. For goodness sake don't tell your missus how much you are losing!

Index

A

B

C

L

M

N

O

P

Q

R

S

T

V

Vanco, 11-14, 18-19, 83, 92, 107, 153, 242-243
Virgin Mobile, 124
Vodafone, 37, 45, 174
Volumes, 43, 54-55, 131-132, 148
VP Group, 13, 98, 149

W

Websites, 33, 40, 75, 108, 228, 244
WHSmith, 96
White Young Green, 77, 159

X

X trades, 56